Legendary Hoosiers

Famous Folks from
the State of Indiana

Nelson Price

Guild Press of Indiana, Inc.

Guild Press of Indiana, Inc.
10665 Andrade Drive
Zionsville, Indiana 46077
317-733-4175

ISBN 1-57860-097-9
Library of Congress Catalog Number 20-01092398

Cover design by Steven D. Armour
Interior and text design by Sheila G. Samson

Printed in China

Lyrics for the songs exerpted in the Cole Porter section are are used by permission of
Robert H. Montgomery, Jr., Trustee of the Cole Porter Musical & Literary Property Trusts.

"You're the Top" © 1934 (Renewed) Warner Bros. Inc.

"In the Still of the Night" © 1937 by Chappell & Co., Inc. Copyright Renewed.

"What is This Thing Called Love?" © 1929 (Renewed) Warner Bros. Inc.

To Susan Bravard—

the Indiana teacher who changed my life.

Contents

Introduction v

Legends in Hoosier History 1

Young Hoosier Legends 45

Legends in Sports 69

Legends in Business and Science 99

Hoosier Entrepreneurs 113

Legends in the Arts 123

Religious and Spiritual Figures 147

Legends in Communications 155

Hoosier Entertainment Legends 163

Bibliography 180

Index 181

Introduction

To many of you, my biggest claim to fame is that I was Reggie Miller's next-door-neighbor in Indianapolis for about three years. No, Reggie and I didn't regularly go out for burgers and Cokes. But we did often chat and joke with each other—the way friendly Hoosiers do—as Reggie was leaving or returning from an Indiana Pacers game. We lived within walking distance of Market Square Arena and a few blocks from the historic Lockerbie neighborhood.

Lockerbie, of course, had been the home decades earlier of another legendary Hoosier, poet James Whitcomb Riley. I memorized Riley poems such as "When the Frost is on the Punkin" as I was growing up on the east side of Indianapolis. While I was learning about the "Hoosier Poet" as a fourth-grader, my family lived just a few blocks from the home of a teenage girl, a Warren Central High School student who would become famous as a TV newswoman. That girl's name is Jane Pauley. I attended every school that Jane did—from Moorhead Elementary School through Indiana University—and felt proud to follow in her footsteps as a fellow "neighborhood kid" interested in communications.

Why do I bring up all of these neighborhood relationships? To point out that legendary Hoosiers grew up among us—and that famous folks of the future undoubtedly are growing up among us today. Maybe in our own families.

Want to be an astronaut? A jazz musician? A novelist, comedian, Olympic champion, or an entrepreneur? Meet some other Hoosiers who chased those dreams—and caught them.

This book was prepared with invaluable research assistance from Wanda Willis.

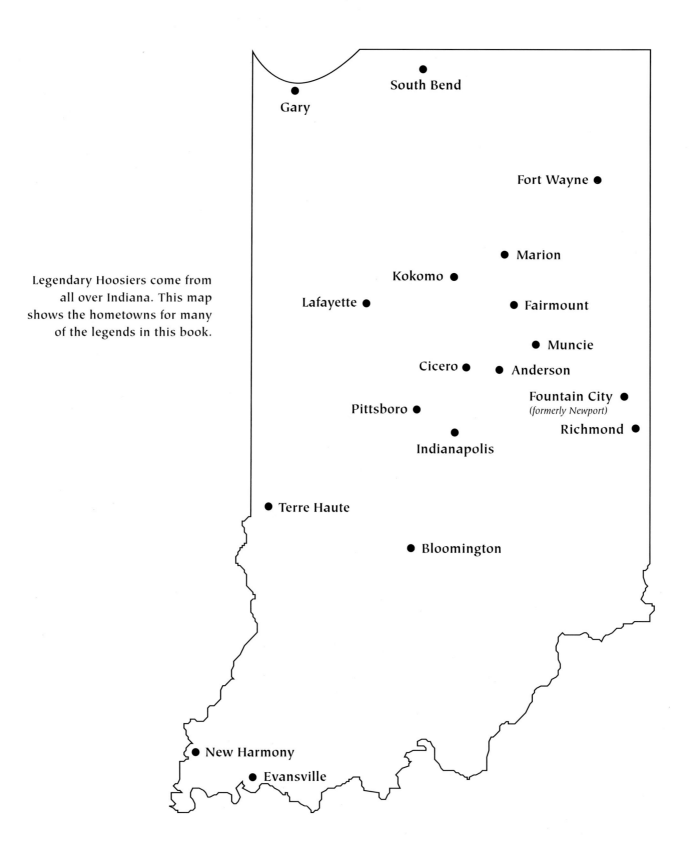

Legendary Hoosiers come from all over Indiana. This map shows the hometowns for many of the legends in this book.

South Bend

Gary

Fort Wayne ●

● Marion

Kokomo ●

Lafayette ●

● Fairmount

● Muncie

Cicero ● ● Anderson

Fountain City ●
(formerly Newport)

Pittsboro ●

● Richmond

●
Indianapolis

● Terre Haute

● Bloomington

● New Harmony

● Evansville

Legends in Hoosier History

Where are the apple trees that Johnny Appleseed planted?

There were no cameras or video equipment in the 1830s to record John Chapman giving apple seedlings to settlers. That makes it difficult to track down exact locations or provide absolute proof about the sites where Appleseed's trees were planted on the frontier.

However, in several regions of Indiana, particularly northern counties, people have long been convinced that certain trees are descended from (that is, related to) seeds planted by Johnny.

Many of these apple trees are in Allen County, where Johnny died. Some of the trees are near what today is the campus of Indiana University-Purdue University at Fort Wayne. Others are in Appleseed Park and Archer Park in Fort Wayne.

Trees in Fulton County, which is in north central Indiana, also might be linked to Johnny Appleseed. Legend has it that Johnny traveled to Fulton County with some Native American friends. Trees near the town of Akron and at various sites in northern Fulton County are believed to have been planted by Appleseed during that visit.

Johnny continues to be remembered in many ways across Indiana. The biggest Appleseed event every year is in September. The Johnny Appleseed Festival in Fort Wayne features pioneer music, food and crafts as well as Native American dances and music. The festival is held in Appleseed Park and surrounding areas of Fort Wayne. More than three hundred thousand people attend the festival and celebrate Johnny, the folk hero who probably never will be forgotten.

This is what Johnny Appleseed (John Chapman) probably looked like as he wandered the wilderness: ragged clothes, stringy hair, and barefooted. Note that he does not have a saucepan on his head. (Indiana Historical Society)

Johnny Appleseed

Many early settlers in the Indiana wilderness laughed at Johnny Apple-seed. They considered him weird—really weird.

His behavior would not seem so odd today, though. Johnny was a vegetarian, which was unusual on the Indiana frontier of the 1830s. He was a pacifist—that is, he objected to war and the use of force. He deeply respected the American Indians. And Johnny, who was a traveling preacher, loved to tell jokes so the settlers would pay attention to his sermons. In Johnny's day, most preachers were very serious and grim.

So who was this mysterious, barefoot man who wandered around in tattered clothes?

First of all, Johnny Appleseed was a real person on the Indiana frontier, not just a Disney cartoon character. His real name was John Chapman; he was born in Massachusetts in 1774.

We know only a few facts about Johnny's childhood in Leominster, a small village in Massachusetts. His mother died when he was two years old. His father remarried, and the Chapman family continued to live in New England, the region of the country that includes Massachusetts and other northeastern states.

Apple Pie from Wild Apple Trees

There are many apple trees growing wild in Indiana. Some huge, old trees may even date back to the time of Johnny Appleseed, though it's not very likely.

If you find a tree with apples on it in the summer, you can make a fine apple pie from the apples. They will be smaller than those in the grocery store and may have spots on them. Apples from wild trees are often tart and tastier than apples you buy in the store. Most of the apples on a tree like this will have good, white flesh inside the peel and no worms, but you'll have to work to pare them. Have an adult work with you to peel the apples and slice them.

Make a double pie crust recipe. (Ready-made pie crusts from the grocer, or crusts made from pie crust mix are also good to use.)

7 cups pared wild apple slices	3 tablespoons flour
1 1/2 cups sugar	2 tablespoons butter
2 teaspoons cinnamon	

Line a 9-inch pie pan with the bottom pie crust. Mix the apples, sugar, cinnamon, and flour and put the mixture into the prepared, unbaked pie shell. Cut up the butter into little pieces and dot over the apple mixture. Cover with top crust and crimp, (close with your fingers in a fancy way). Make four steam escape holes with fork tines on the top of the crust.

Bake at 375 degrees for 45 minutes, or until the juices the pie makes are thickened and coming out of the holes on the top of the pie. Serve with vanilla ice cream, thick cream (the old-fashioned Hoosier way), or cheese à la New England.

So what brought Johnny to the Indiana frontier?

The answer begins many years before Johnny was born. In the 1700s, English traders and settlers began filtering into the wilderness areas that became the states of Indiana, Ohio, Illinois, and Michigan. In the 1760s, the British defeated the French, who had controlled the Midwest frontier; as a result, more English pioneers moved west. Following the Revolutionary War (1775–1783), the pioneers came in a rush.

John Chapman—or Appleseed—eventually welcomed them with apple seedlings. He had grown up to become a traveling preacher of the Swedenborgian (Church of the New Jerusalem) faith. So Johnny headed west not only to give apple seedlings to the pioneers, but also to give them scriptures—including chapters of the Bible.

Chapman, who never married, died in the Fort Wayne area in 1845.

What did he contribute to our state's history?

Johnny Appleseed demonstrated a sense of neighborliness and religious faith that lonely settlers cherished. He also brought the latest news, and, of course, the apple—the fruit whose sauces and pies added to the comfort, happiness and health of people on the Hoosier frontier.

Did Johnny Appleseed really wear a saucepan?

Maybe you have seen the Disney Studios cartoon version of Johnny Appleseed. In the movie *Melody Time*, young Appleseed—or John Chapman, which was his real name—wears a cooking pot on his head, kind of like a baseball cap. Experts, though, doubt that he really did that.

More than eighty eyewitnesses on the frontier described Johnny Appleseed. Only two of them mentioned a saucepan.

"How come so many people who wrote about seeing Johnny Appleseed never mentioned it?" says Hank Fincken, an Indianapolis playwright who has studied and portrayed the folk hero. "If you wore a pot on your head, it would be the first thing everyone would report."

This cartoon version of Johnny Appleseed is from Walt Disney's movie *Melody Time* (1948). Although the real Johnny Appleseed loved animals as shown here, experts doubt that he actually wore a saucepan. (© Walt Disney, courtesy of Photofest)

The Vincennes

Two of the first legendary Hoosiers actually came from Canada. They were father and son, explorers of French heritage. Both men suffered horrible deaths—one from nature, the other from other men.

The father and son were both known as the **Sieur de Vincennes**. We will call them Vincennes Sr. and Jr.

They lived in the 1600s and early 1700s, long before Indiana was a state or even a territory; it was just a wilderness. Beginning in the 1600s, the French sent priests and explorers to settle the frontier that was the middle part of America.

The first Sieur de Vincennes was born in **Quebec, Canada**, in 1668. At that time, Canada and the middle of America—including what would become Indiana—were known as "New France."

In his hometown of Quebec, Vincennes Sr. attended a Catholic seminary, a school for young men training to be priests. His real name was Jean-Baptiste Bissot. (Sieur de Vincennes was a title that Bissot and his son were given later in their lives. "Sieur" was a common short version of "monsieur," the French form of "mister.")

Vincennes Sr. came to the Indiana wilderness to encourage fur trading between the French and the Native Americans of the Wea and Miami tribes. The priest was respected and liked by many of the Indians, and he urged the Miami to become Catholics. He became the father of seven children before dying during the bitter winter of 1718–1719.

One of those seven children, Sieur de Vincennes Jr., was born in 1700. His real name was Francois-Marie Bissot. He continued his father's work among the Miami, helping them in the fur trade. To give the traders a place to live, the French founded the first permanent white settlement in Indiana. Known as Fort Ouiatenan, it was a remote outpost near what is now the city of Lafayette. Vincennes Jr. was put in charge of the fort in 1722.

Because of his outstanding record there, Vincennes Jr. earned the right to build a new fort on the Wabash River—Fort Vincennes, what is today the city of **Vincennes**. Construction began in the early 1730s. Slowly, the village sprang up, complete with rough cottages for settlers, taverns for fur traders and pigs running in the dirt roads. The village of Vincennes was finished in 1732.

Soon afterward, Vincennes Jr. celebrated two joyous events. He was promoted to lieutenant in the French army, and he married his wife, Marie. Within a few years, the young couple had two daughters. Like his father, Vincennes Jr. was respected by the Wea and Miami who lived nearby.

Then, in 1736, came a disastrous event that resulted in Vincennes Jr.'s tragic death.

Far away in the south, the French governor of Louisiana was planning massive attacks against an Indian tribe called the Chickasaw. The French governor needed help—manpower—from fellow colonial settlers in Indiana and Illinois. He asked Vincennes Jr. to come south with all of the men he could round up—French settlers and Indian braves—to help attack the Chickasaw.

The decision to attack was a big mistake. Alerted to the movements of the French group, Chickasaw leaders gathered a group of more than four hundred warriors. They fell in a fury upon the Northerners, who were forced to flee.

The Chickasaw took several prisoners, including Vincennes Jr. and a priest. The prisoners were taken to an isolated Chickasaw village in what is now the state of Mississippi. In the middle of the village, the warriors chanted, sang hymns, and built a huge fire.

According to some accounts, some of the prisoners, including Vincennes Jr. and the priest, were burned at a stake. Other witnesses said years later that the prisoners were tossed into the massive bonfire.

In any case, news of the horrible death of Vincennes Jr. spread north to the French forts and Indian villages along the Wabash River. People were devastated. The new village of Fort Vincennes had lost its beloved commander and many of its adult men.

It was no wonder, though, that the Chickasaw were angry enough to order the deaths of their prisoners. Many Frenchmen had been robbing corn from Indian villages in the south, taking food that was meant to feed their women and children through the winter. Many Indians also resented the French for traveling or settling on their lands; they feared the whites would break their promises to pay for the property that they took.

So Vincennes Jr. was a tragic victim in what was essentially a war between two cultures: white settlers and the Indians. It was a war that would last a long time.

This is how the burning death in 1736 of Sieur de Vincennes Jr. (Francois-Marie Bissot) may have looked. The drawing was done by famous Hoosier artist Will Vawter. (Byron Lewis Library/Vincennes University)

George Rogers Clark

There were only one hundred and seventy men in **George Rogers Clark**'s ragtag volunteer army in the winter of 1779. And the American freedom fighters were exhausted, wet, hungry, and nearly out of supplies by the time they reached **Vincennes**.

George Rogers Clark (1752–1818) was a fearless and aggressive frontiersman. He had waded with his men through icy, waist-high water to reach Vincennes, which had been captured by the British and renamed Fort Sackville. In the waning days of the Revolutionary War, Clark was determined to take back Vincennes for the Americans, even though they were outnumbered.

"Great things have been affected by a few men well conducted," he wrote Virginia Governor Patrick Henry.

The British at Vincennes refused to surrender. Clark—a tall, red-haired, commanding leader—then paraded his men in such a way that the British redcoats and townspeople of Vincennes thought he was leading an army of one thousand people—not just one hundred and seventy.

After one day of fighting, the British leader at Vincennes, Colonel Henry Hamilton, surrendered to Clark. The new American flag was raised over the

Frontier fighter George Rogers Clark, as he looked late in life. (Bass Photo Company Collection/Indiana Historical Society)

fort; this was the first major American victory in the West during the Revolutionary War. Because of Clark, America included what is today the Midwest instead of just the East Coast.

News about the success of Clark's frontier army reached the British and American leaders as they met in Paris, France, for peace talks. They were debating the location of the western boundary of the new United States of America. Clark's victory helped the Americans win major agreements from the British in the Treaty of 1783. Be-cause of this, Clark eventually became known as "the father of the Northwest Territory."

In 1784, five years after his triumph at Vincennes, Clark founded the city of **Clarksville**—the first Indiana town founded after Vincennes. (The land for the town had been granted to Clark and some of his men as a reward for their bravery.)

George Rogers Clark had grown up in a family destined for fame. His brother, William, became one of the American West's best-known explorers. He was the "Clark" half of the famous Lewis and Clark duo.

Despite his glory as a frontiersman and military leader, George Rogers Clark did not have a comfortable life— or a perfect reputation. He has been called "ruthless" for his treatment of American Indians, some of whom he ordered scalped to scare the British. He also struggled with money problems and alcoholism. Many described Clark as a bitter man when he died in 1818 at his sister's home in Louisville, Kentucky.

In this mural, George Rogers Clark—"The Hero of Vincennes"—leads his men through an icy stream in February 1779. The mural, painted by F. C. Yohn, is in the George Rogers Clark Memorial in Vincennes, Indiana. (Indiana Historical Society)

Tecumseh and the Prophet

Two of the most famous Native Americans in Indiana history were brothers. One was a brilliant, controversial leader who dreamed of creating a massive, united Indian nation. The other was a colorful religious leader whose mistakes and downfall had an impact on the fate of his people.

Tecumseh and the Prophet were Shawnee Indians. Their father was a respected Shawnee chief who lived in a village in western Ohio. According to Native American legend, at the very moment when Tecumseh was born—probably in 1768—a panther, one of the spirit world's fiercest creatures, passed across the sky in the form of a meteor.

"Tecumseh's people interpreted the sign to mean they were witnessing the birth of an extraordinary person who would do wonderful things in his lifetime for his people," according to *Kohkumthena's Grandchildren*, a book by Shawnee author Dark Rain Thom. "[Tecumseh] was brought up aware that he was expected to be better than his peers because the Creator had something special for him to do with his life."

His brother's name at birth was Tenskwatawa, but he would become famous as the Prophet. According to

Distinguished-looking Chief Tecumseh, Shawnee leader and warrior. (Indiana Historical Society)

some accounts, Tecumseh and the Prophet were the two surviving brothers of a set of triplets. Yet other versions of family history say the triplets, including the Prophet, were Tecumseh's younger brothers.

Their village in Ohio was surrounded by towering beech, sassafras, elm, and walnut trees. Many of the trees were more than thirty feet tall.

The sassafras trees sometimes perfumed the Shawnee village, making it sweet smelling when there was a breeze.

Tecumseh and the Prophet had an older brother named Chiksika. The boys' father was killed in 1774 during a battle with frontiersmen.

Legend has it that the dying father whispered to his oldest son—fourteen-year-old Chiksika—that he must never make peace with white settlers and must oversee his younger brothers' training as warriors.

Tecumseh was built for that. He grew to become muscular, slim, and straight. At his full adult height, he stood about five feet, ten inches (fairly tall in those days) and had a proud bearing and piercing, hazel eyes.

Often riding along with Chiksika, Tecumseh joined in small raids against white settlers. His fury at whites increased when his beloved Chiksika was killed during a battle in 1788.

Tecumseh and the Prophet settled in the Indiana frontier about 1800. The brothers built a village called Pro-phetstown on the banks of the Tippecanoe River.

The Prophet had a reputation among his people as an alcoholic. But in 1805, after he slipped into a coma and recovered, he claimed he had seen "visions" during a near-death experience. He proclaimed himself the messenger of the "Great Spirit." He began to travel, preaching his "gospel" about mistreated Indians to various tribes.

Tecumseh was away from Proph-etstown even more than his brother was. He worked to create a vast Indian nation that would stretch from the Allegheny Mountains in the east to the Everglades in Florida and the Ozark Mountains. Blessed with dazzling speaking skills, Tecumseh traveled to Indian tribes to persuade them to join his nation and throw out the whites.

Tecumseh was on one of these trips in 1811 when William Henry Harrison, governor of the Indiana Territory, and an army of about one thousand men marched up the Wabash River. They camped beside the Tippecanoe River a few miles from Prophetstown.

Against what he knew would have been his brother's wishes, the Prophet decided to attack. At dawn on November 7, the Prophet and his warriors surprised Harrison and his army. Although the Americans suffered staggering casualties in bloody, hand-to-hand fighting during the Battle of Tippecanoe, they managed to drive off the Indians. Then Harrison and his soldiers marched to the empty Pro-phetstown and burned it to the ground.

Tecumseh was horrified when he returned in January of 1812 and saw the ashes of his village. He feared his dream of a pan-American nation of Indians was shattered.

Once again, he vowed revenge on the whites. He also denounced the Prophet as a disgrace. Some outraged Shawnee even wanted to kill the Prophet, who moaned at his brother's feet. Tecumseh spared the Prophet from death, but turned on his heel and walked away from him. Depressed and homeless, the Prophet lived about twenty-five more years, eventually dying in the West in the mid-1830s.

The Prophet—Tecumseh's flamboyant brother, religious leader, and warrior. (Indiana Historical Society)

Meanwhile, Tecumseh drew on his inner strength and gathered his warriors. He sensed the approaching War of 1812 between the Americans and the British. Tecumseh concluded that joining the English would be the only way to drive the Americans from Indian hunting grounds.

So Tecumseh and his warriors moved across the border to Canada. Once there, Tecumseh gathered perhaps the most powerful force ever commanded by a Native American. Along with British troops, Tecumseh and his warriors swooped south and captured Detroit in 1812. The next year, Tecumseh joined a British invasion of Ohio.

But the Indians and British were forced by Harrison and his men to retreat to Ontario, Canada, along the Thames River. In October of 1813, Tecumseh was killed during the Battle of the Thames.

Upon the death of the fiery Shawnee leader, even his old enemy Harrison praised his talents. Harrison wrote that Tecumseh was "one of those geniuses which spring up occasionally to produce revolutions and overturn the established order of things. If it were not for the vicinity of the United States, he would perhaps be the founder of an Empire that would rival in glory Mexico or Peru."

Did Tecumseh and William Henry Harrison almost duke it out?

The two great rivals of the Old Northwest almost drew their weapons—or may have been about to swing their fists—at each other.

It would have been an unusual clash in 1810 because both men were proud, distinguished leaders, and the setting was the lawn of Grouseland, the plantation-style mansion of the governor of the Indiana Territory.

That governor was thirty-seven-year-old William Henry Harrison. The other leader was Tecumseh, the regal, fortyish Shawnee chief.

Both men were determined to save the cultures of their boyhoods. On a hot day in August 1810, Governor Harrison and Tecumseh met on the lawn of Grouseland with several of their trusted aides. Tecumseh was angered by the Treaty of Fort Wayne, which Harrison had negotiated with other Indian leaders two years earlier.

Through an interpreter, Tecumseh, who was wearing buckskin, accused Harrison of pitting Indians against each other. He claimed that Harrison and other white leaders took advantage of the Indians to obtain "ownership" of three million acres.

"Brother, you ought to know what you are doing with the Indians," Tecumseh told Harrison. "It is a very bad thing, and we do not like it . . .

"Brother, do not believe that I came here to get presents from you. If you offer us any, we will not take [them]. By taking goods from you, you will hereafter say that with them you purchased another piece of land from us."

Land was like the air and water, Tecumseh argued, his voice rising. It was a common possession of all Indians, not a single tribe. That's why Harrison's "purchase" of land from some Indian chiefs was not valid or legal, Tecumseh said.

Harrison argued back, saying the other Indian chiefs had known what they were doing when they gave him the land. According to some accounts, Tecumseh then called the governor a "liar" to his face. Other versions say an Indian chief who sided with the whites deliberately misinterpreted the Shawnee leader's words.

In any case, Tecumseh and Harrison glared at each other and nearly started to brawl. Alarmed, some of the governor's soldiers drew their guns. But the confrontation ended when both leaders realized that a tussle between them would solve nothing for the thousands of people who depended on each of them.

William Henry Harrison

This painting of William Henry Harrison was done in 1814 and hangs in Grouseland, Harrison's mansion in Vincennes. (Indiana Historical Society)

He was the ninth president of the United States and the first to die in office. But **William Henry Harrison** was a youthful twenty-six years old when he was named to a powerful job that brought him to the **Indiana Territory.**

It was 1800, and young William Henry Harrison was appointed the first governor of the Indiana Territory, a vast wilderness area. (Indiana did not become a state until sixteen years later.)

Harrison and his wife Anna moved their family—which eventually included ten children—to **Vincennes**, the capital of the Indiana Territory. On a three-hundred-acre estate near the Wabash River, Harrison built a mansion that he called Grouseland.

He wanted to copy the plantation life of his boyhood. William Henry Harrison (1773–1841) had grown up on a plantation in Virginia. His father had been one of the signers of the Declaration of Independence in 1776, so Harrison considered himself a "child of the Revolution." His boyhood plantation, called Berkeley, had a mill for grinding corn and wheat, stables for cattle and horses, chicken coops, a blacksmith shop, and a carriage shed. Young William Henry was taught by private tutors; about one hundred slaves worked for the Harrison family at Berkeley.

Probably to please his parents, Harrison spent a year studying to be a doctor. His comfortable world was shattered when his father suddenly died. As the youngest son, William Henry inherited no land from the estate. (At that time, all of the property of wealthy families often was given only to the oldest son.)

So William Henry Harrison had to scramble to support himself. He joined the military in 1791. Even though he was just eighteen years old, Harrison was able to recruit about eighty men to risk their lives fighting Indians in the wilderness; the men were paid two dollars a month.

Over the next seven years, Harrison rose to the rank of captain. His success in fighting Indians resulted in his appointment as the Indiana Territory's first governor.

Upon arriving in Vincennes, Harrison was shocked by what he considered the crude behavior of many white settlers. In the booming frontier towns, many men traveled to the wilderness to kill Indians at random. At first, Harrison tried to stop what he considered lawless behavior. Eventually, he just gave up trying to have white settlers arrested for the murders of Native Americans.

Meanwhile, Harrrison considered himself a strong negotiator with Native American tribes in the Indiana Ter-

ritory. In 1809, he negotiated the Treaty of Fort Wayne in which the Delaware, Miami, Potawatomi, and Eel River Indians gave up about three million acres of land in exchange for yearly payments of money. The treaty angered Tecumseh, the famous Shawnee leader, who became Harrison's lifelong enemy.

When Tecumseh was away from his village, called Prophetstown, Harrison led an army that marched up the Wabash River. Tecumseh's brother, the Prophet, ordered a surprise attack on Harrison's troops. But Harrison's men, who had been sleeping on their weapons, launched a counterattack that became known as the Battle of Tippecanoe. "Old Tip," as Harrison came to be called, led his troops into Prophetstown and burned it.

During the War of 1812, Harrison pulled off more military victories against the British and Indians. Praised as a war hero, he settled in Ohio and managed a farm.

While living in Ohio, he ran for U.S. president twice—losing in 1836, but winning four years later in 1840. Despite the fact that Harrison had grown up on a lavish plantation in Virginia and had lived in a mansion in Indiana, he campaigned for the White House as a humble farmer from Ohio. His crusade for the presidency was called "the log cabin campaign."

"Old Tip" was sixty-seven years old by the time he won election to the White House—and he didn't get to stay there long. In March of 1841, he gave one of the longest inaugural speeches in American history. Exhausted, he died a month later of pneumonia.

Footnote

Because William Henry Harrison was an Ohio farmer when he was elected to the White House, he is not considered a president from Indiana. But he had a link to the first (and, so far, only) Hoosier elected president. In 1888, more than forty-seven years after William Henry Harrison died, his grandson became president. He was Benjamin Harrison of Indianapolis. For more information about him, see the article about Benjamin and Caroline Harrison later in this book.

Little Turtle

One of the greatest military leaders in Native American history, **Little Turtle**, was born in 1751 near the present city of Fort Wayne.

Little Turtle was a member of the Miami tribe of Indians. He lived in a Miami village known as **Kekionga**. Located on the banks of the St. Joseph River and very near two other rivers— the Maumee and the St. Mary's— Kekionga was an Indian village that was, in some ways, similar to European villages of the era. The Miami in Kekionga mingled with traders and various visitors from other cultures, particularly the French and British. Some of the residents of Kekionga even spoke French. Occasionally, a French trader would marry a Miami woman.

The Miami Indians, who were known for being hard working, raised several varieties of corn, their favorite crop. They stored their corn in pits lined with bark from trees; sometimes these pits were six feet deep. The Miami also raised squash, melons, and pumpkins. (They usually settled their villages on the banks of rivers like the St. Joseph because the riverbank soil was rich and would support a variety of plants.) In Miami villages like Kekionga, the women were the ones who harvested the crops.

Little Turtle, leader of the Miami.
(Indiana Historical Society)

The Miami chose leaders who were calm and mild-mannered. For many years while Little Turtle was growing up, life in Kekionga was pleasant. The biggest problems were occasional epidemics of illnesses such as smallpox and measles. The Miami played a game with wooden balls and sticks that was similar to the modern game of lacrosse. It was very rough, and a match might last all day.

In summer and autumn, Miami women and children would gather fruits, nuts, and berries to eat. They also gathered leaves, barks, roots, and fruits to make various medicines. Miami families ate a lot of duck, chicken, turkey and quail; they didn't tend to fish as much as other Indian tribes.

In the late fall, Miami men would leave on hunting trips. They hunted deer, bear, bison, and elk. Sometimes they traded the meat and skins with the French and British. (As Little Turtle was growing up during the mid-1700s, fewer and fewer of these large animals could be found in the Indiana wilderness. So the Miami also began hunting smaller animals such as raccoons and opossum.)

Later in life, Little Turtle described Kekionga as that "glorious gate which the Miamis had the happiness to own, and through which all the good words of their chiefs had to pass from the north to the south, and from the east to the west."

Little Turtle's first burst of fame came in 1780, when the French attacked the Miami and other tribes living near the Maumee River.

When Little Turtle heard of the invasion, he rallied an army of Miami warriors to pursue the French. Although the Indians were greatly outnumbered, they defeated the French by surrounding their camp and attacking after nightfall. They killed the entire brigade of white men.

Ten years later in 1790, Little Turtle and his warriors killed six hundred and eighty soldiers of the new country of the United States of America.

In response, Congress ordered a general in the Indiana Territory—Brigadier General Josiah Harmer—to raise a force of men to destroy the Miami. Little Turtle and his warriors turned back the initial force in 1791, killing about nine hundred men. This victory by Little Turtle was the largest single battlefield defeat—ever—of U.S. soldiers by Native Americans.

Little Turtle's triumph was short-lived, though. A Revolutionary War hero named "Mad" Anthony Wayne (1745–1796) analyzed Little Turtle's warfare strategies. Then Wayne gathered a huge force of five thousand men. Many among his ragtag group were beggars and criminals from the streets and prisons of Eastern cities.

Wayne and his unusual force of men took on the Miami in a battle near Toledo, Ohio, and not far from the site of Fort Wayne (which is named for "Mad" Anthony). In the Battle of Fallen Timbers in 1794, the Miami fought courageously. The strength of Wayne's force, however, eventually forced them to flee.

Things happened quickly after that. Little Turtle struck a friendly agreement with the Americans. Then, the year after the Battle of Fallen Timbers, "Mad" Anthony built Fort Wayne.

For the rest of his life, Little Turtle lived at his lodge in northeastern Indiana. He continued to be a respected leader who urged improvements in the quality of life and morals of Native Americans. Little Turtle died at his lodge in 1812.

Johann George Rapp and Robert Owen

For thousands of years, people have dreamed of Utopia—the perfect society. In Indiana, the place selected by more than one group to try to create Utopia was New Harmony. It's a scenic village in the hills of southwestern Indiana near the Wabash River.

The first leader to arrive in New Harmony to build his Utopia was a German religious crusader named **Johann George Rapp** (1757–1847). Rapp left his homeland because he objected to many of the teachings of the Lutheran church as well as laws in Germany. For example, Rapp didn't believe in the baptism of infants and didn't believe in serving in the military. With his followers, who were called "Rappites," Rapp traveled far away to the Indiana wilderness and New Harmony in 1814.

Here, the Rappites practiced "perfect" living as they waited for the Second Coming of Christ. They didn't even have tombs in their cemetery—they were convinced that the "dead" bodies would be getting up soon! Men and women in New Harmony lived separately in large dormitories and farmed in fields nearby. They were good businessmen and shipped flatboats full of wheat, corn, and pigs down the Wabash River, then to the Mississippi River to New Orleans.

Robert Owen, Utopia seeker and leader at New Harmony. (Bass Photo Company Collection/ Indiana Historical Society)

Robert Dale Owen, oldest son of Robert Owen and a politician in early Indiana. He helped revise the state constitution in the early 1850s. Robert Dale Owen's brother, David Dale Owen, became Indiana's first state geologist. (Indiana Historical Society)

Under the Rappites, the village grew to nine hundred people and flourished for ten years. Rapp, though, concluded that his followers had become complacent—lazy—and decided to move to Pennsylvania in 1824.

The Rappites sold their village that year to the second Utopia-seeker, a wealthy Scottish businessman named Robert Owen (1771–1858). Born in Wales, he had attended school only until age ten. But by hard work, Owen rose to become the manager of a large cotton mill while only in his teens.

After moving to Scotland, Owen became a social reformer, crusading to improve schools and working conditions. He built schools and reading rooms for his employees and assigned "work monitors" to make sure his workers were productive and happy.

By the time he bought New Harmony from the Rappites, Robert Owen was fifty-three years old—but still bursting with energy. Hoping to make New Harmony free of poverty and inequality, Owen brought scientists, teachers and poets to the Indiana village.

Once again, New Harmony started out well. But the Utopia didn't last. Villagers bickered among themselves, squabbling about everything from religion to daily chores. No one, for example, wanted to fork the manure.

The Utopia—which had been called "the experiment on the Wabash River"—collapsed in 1827. Many of the sturdy, historic buildings in New Harmony have survived, however. They are fascinating to tour.

Fun facts

- Under the Rappites, the Indiana village was known as "Harmonie." Robert Owen renamed it New Harmony.

- Robert Owen brought scientists, poets, teachers and other distinguished Europeans to New Harmony on a keelboat called the "Boatload of Knowledge."

- One of Owen's sons, David Dale Owen (1807–1860), became Indiana's first state geologist. Going from county to county, David Dale Owen examined fossils and documented the soil, water and rocks, including limestone and coal in southern Indiana.

Other Utopias

One of the first famous people to think about what a Utopia (or perfect society) should be was an ancient Greek philosopher named Plato.

He lived about 400 B.C.E. (Before the Christian Era), and wrote about the ideal Greek state. Plato valued wisdom and knowledge above almost all else. In Plato's version of Utopia, men and women would love learning. There would be open discussion of ideas—and good ideas would be tested to see if they held up.

Another famous man with a vision of Utopia was an Englishman named Sir Thomas More (1478–1535). In his Utopia, people would love education and hold firm to their religious faith.

What is your idea of Utopia?

Chief Menominee

One of the worst tragedies in Indiana history was the Trail of Death.

A key figure in the 1838 tragedy was **Chief Menominee**, the leader of the Potawatomi tribe of Native Americans in northern Indiana. In the early 1800s, when our state still was a wilderness known as the Indiana Territory, the Potawatomi held practically all of the land north of the Wabash River—that is, one-fourth of what eventually became Indiana.

Chief Menominee was known for his strongly spiritual nature and leadership skills. Like other Potawatomi, he also was known for his colorful clothes. Instead of the buckskin and war paint associated with some Native American tribes, the Potawatomi preferred ruffled shirts, jewelry and pants with dangling ribbons.

Chief Menominee probably was born in 1791. He became a Roman Catholic and was a peacemaker by nature. However, he was determined to hold on to what remained of the Potawatomi's land in northern Indiana after a series of treaties with white settlers.

The settlers, led by **General John Tipton** (1786–1839), were pressuring the Potawatomi to give up their land in northern Indiana. The land that the Potawatomi held was some of the last in the state occupied by Indians. Because American settlers were pouring into the Midwest, sending Indians west to places like Kansas and putting them on reservations seemed the best solution.

"We need the land; it is our destiny," pioneer families cried. It didn't seem to matter that the Native Americans had traveled over or camped on the woodlands for thousands of years.

Farmers and their families eventually surrounded the Potawatomi settlement in the "Twin Lakes" region of northern Indiana. As the Potawatomi went to get water from creeks or hunt the few remaining deer, farm girls in sunbonnets stared at them, and young boys pointed rifles to taunt them. The settlers around Twin Lakes began to clamor for the reservation lands, threatening violence if they could not have the property.

Finally, federal officials decided they could not hold back the settlers. The Potawatomi had to go! Federal officials claimed Chief Menominee had signed away his land in a treaty. The conflict between the leaders of the two cultures—General Tipton and Chief Menominee—eventually led to the Trail of Death.

In the summer of 1838—when the state of Indiana was just twenty-one years old—there was a standoff near Logansport between white leaders and Potawatomi chiefs. Chief Menominee refused to leave his village, claiming he had never signed a treaty or sold his land.

The chief defied an order from Indiana's governor, David Wallace, to move. The Potawatomi said they didn't want to leave "the graves of our children"—the land where they had buried their young. As the conflict became tense, Chief Menominee even met with the president of the United States, Martin Van Buren.

"I have not sold my lands," Chief Menominee said in a speech after meeting with the president. "I will not sell them."

In September of 1838, soldiers under General Tipton's command arrived at Menominee's village in the Twin Lakes region. The soldiers were determined to force the 859 Potawatomi men, women, and children to leave.

The Potawatomi paid a final visit to their graveyard. Then Tipton and his soldiers led the Native Americans on a nine-hundred-mile march to Kansas—the Trail of Death. Chief Menominee and some other men were put in cages like animals. During the trip, which took sixty-two days, dozens of Indians died from disease and exhaustion.

This statue of Chief Menominee stands near his beloved Twin Lakes in northern Indiana.

General John Tipton, military leader. (Tippecanoe County Historical Association)

"It was a sad and mournful spectacle," wrote one eyewitness, "to (watch) these children of the forest slowly retiring from the home of their childhood . . ."

The Potawatomi who survived the Trail of Death were ordered to live on a Western reservation. Chief Menominee died in Kansas in 1841.

Eventually, most of the Potawatomi were taken to Oklahoma. In recent years, though, many Potawatomi have returned to Indiana. Their tragic and courageous story is remembered every September in Fulton County during the Trail of Courage Living History Festival.

Tipton County in north-central Indiana is named after General Tipton. Before the Trail of Death, Tipton had played a key role in founding the cities of Columbus, Logansport, and Huntington. Tipton also served as a U.S. senator from Indiana.

A statue of Chief Menominee stands near the Twin Lakes he loved so much. The statue is surrounded by cornfields—just as Chief Menominee and his people had been.

Menominee's speech after a visit with the president

In 1838, as the conflict heated up between the Potawatomi Indians and white settlers in Indiana, Chief Menominee met with President Martin Van Buren. After his visit with the President of the United States—and one month before the Potawatomi leader was removed by force from Indiana—Menominee said in a speech to white and Indian political leaders:

"The president does not know the truth. He, like me, has been imposed upon. . . . He would not drive me from my home and the graves of my tribe, and my children, who have gone to the Great Spirit, nor allow you to tell me your braves will take me, tied like a dog. When [the president] knows the truth, he will leave me to my own.

"I have not sold my lands. I will not sell them."

Levi and Catharine Coffin

Beginning about twenty years before the American Civil War, a silent, invisible "transportation system" developed across Northern and border states.

Set up by homeowners who sympathized with slaves and wanted to help them escape from the South, the transportation system became known as the Underground Railroad. Often traveling in the dark of night, slaves headed north, sometimes as far as Canada, to live in freedom. As they fled, they found refuge in the homes of friendly people.

One house on the Underground Railroad was in a tiny town called Newport in eastern Indiana. This house became the stopover for so many escaped slaves in the 1840s that it was nicknamed "the Grand Central Station" of the Underground Railroad. (Grand Central Station is a bustling train/subway station in New York City.)

The house—a red brick, two-story home with a basement and a secret hiding place—was owned by Levi and Catharine Coffin. The Coffins were Quakers who felt passionately that slavery was wrong; they also felt that all of the other Quakers in town should join their crusade against it.

Because Levi Coffin (1798–1877)

Motivated by their Quaker beliefs, Levi and Catharine Coffin helped thousands of runaway slaves escape before the Civil War. (Courtesy of The Levi Coffin House Association)

was a prosperous merchant—he controlled a bank, a flour mill and several stores in Newport—townspeople found it hard to say no to him.

Catharine (1803–1881) was just as dedicated as her husband. She persuaded her friends to gather around a spinning wheel in the Coffin home, where they prepared yarn to weave blankets and clothes for the runaway slaves.

So where did these nightly visitors hide in the home?

The Coffin house had a second-floor room that usually served as a bedroom for two maids who helped Levi and Catharine care for their six children. The maids' bedroom had a small, secret door on one wall. The door opened to a narrow crawl space, or "hideaway." As many as fourteen slaves could huddle in it if a slave-owner showed up at the house, searching for them. (The "hideaway" room—along with the rest of the Coffin house—is open to the public for tours. It's a popular destination for school field trips.)

Levi and Catharine Coffin helped runaway slaves in other ways, too. They convinced one of their friends, the town doctor in Newport, to treat ex-slaves who had been wounded during their escapes or nighttime flights. The Coffins also helped start schools for newly free black people who decided to settle in Indiana.

The Hannah House

The home of Levi and Catharine Coffin wasn't the only Indiana house on the legendary "Underground Railroad." Still standing on the south side of Indianapolis is a two-story, brick farmhouse built by a Quaker named Alexander Hannah (1821–1885). It's a house that's rumored to be haunted—by the ghosts of slaves.

Escaped slaves would hide in the cold, dark cellar of the mansion, which Hannah had built about 1858.

According to folklore, several slaves arrived one chilly evening in early spring, when the ground was still covered with snow. The slaves hid in the cellar until the next morning, when Hannah and his family could make arrangements for them to be taken in a hay wagon to the next stop on the Underground Railroad.

Shivering in the clammy cellar, the slaves huddled for warmth. Hannah brought them fresh water and cold meats as well as lanterns so they could see in the darkness.

Exact details of what happened next are unknown. Apparently, a lantern was knocked over. Fire erupted. The Hannah family and their servants were awakened by screams and the crackling sound of flames. They rushed to the cellar to try to put the fire out. The slaves, though, had been trapped, and several died.

Hannah wanted to give the slaves a proper burial, but he couldn't because that would reveal the secret hiding place. So, according to folklore, the slaves were buried in the cellar.

The house on Madison Avenue and National Avenue sat vacant for many years after Hannah died. Later owners said they would occasionally hear the sound of breaking glass from the cellar.

Visitors reported feeling "watched" when they went down to the cellar. Sometimes doors would open and close. And some people even reported hearing moans and screams from the cellar. They also reported catching glimpses of a shadowy figure—a man in old-fashioned clothes and large, mutton-chop whiskers or sideburns.

According to legend, this is the ghost of Alexander Hannah. Some people think the house is haunted, that the shattered glass is the sound of a lantern being overturned—and that the moans are those of the poor, trapped slaves from long ago.

By doing all of this, the Coffins risked going to jail. Under the Fugitive Slave Act of 1793, all Americans—even Northerners—were required to turn in runaway slaves. Helping an escaped slave was like being involved in a robbery.

In 1847, Levi and Catherin Coffin moved from Newport to Ohio. They settled in Cincinnati, where they hoped to pursue their antislavery crusade—and their business dealings—in a larger city.

Experts credit the Coffins with helping a total of two thousand slaves find freedom.

Did you know?

- The town in Wayne County where Levi and Catharine Coffin lived in the 1840s no longer is called Newport. After the Coffins left, the village had to change its name to avoid confusion with a second Indiana town that had named itself Newport. The village with the Coffin home is now known as Fountain City.

- The Coffins' anti-slavery crusade was motivated by their religious beliefs. "The Bible, in bidding us to feed the hungry and clothe the naked, said nothing about color," Levi Coffin wrote in 1876.

- Levi Coffin said he first became horrified by slavery when he was seven years old. In North Carolina, where he grew up, Levi was chopping wood with his father when they saw a group of slaves pass by in chains. One dejected slave explained that they had been chained so they wouldn't escape and try to find their wives and children. Young Levi thought about how terrible it would be if his father were taken away and chained.

- When they died, Levi and Catharine Coffin were nearly penniless. After they moved to Cincinnati, the Coffins helped hundreds of slaves escape, but their businesses failed there in the 1850s and 1860s.

One of the key Northern stops on the "Underground Railroad," the Levi Coffin house has a secret room upstairs where slaves could hide. The house is in the Wayne County town of Fountain City, which was known as Newport when the Coffins lived there. (Courtesy of The Levi Coffin House Association)

Legendary Civil War Regiments

Fourteenth Indiana Volunteers

Although Civil War regiments aren't individuals, they often thought of themselves as legends, and indeed a few Indiana regiments were legends in the days of the war and beyond.

The Fourteenth Indiana was perhaps the best reported on of any regiment in the state. It would have been considered a "media darling" today. In April and May of 1861, many small and larger towns in the Hoosier State organized regiments of young men to go to the war near Washington, D.C., because it was believed the South would march up to the nation's capital and take it right away.

The Fourteenth Indiana, which had ten companies from the south and central part of Indiana, quickly organized a thousand men to help "Mr. Lincoln save Washington City." They were the first regiment in the state to agree to stay for three years; most Americans believed the war would be over in three months. How wrong those folks were!

After brief training in Indianapolis, the Fourteenth got on trains in July of 1861 and went to western Virginia, which was then seceding from Virginia, part of the Confederacy. They stood in reserve at the first land battle of the Civil War, Rich Mountain, and then settled in on a high, cold mountain in what was soon to be West Virginia. They almost froze in the cold winds and snow, because the only uniforms they had fell to pieces, being made of a cheap gray material called "shoddy."

Soon, with new blue uniforms, they were fighting in famous battles: the Seven Days Battles near Richmond, Anietam, Fredericksburg, Chancellorsville, Gettysburg, and the Wilderness.

They were covered by local papers in places like Vincennes and Terre Haute and Evansville, which sent their own war correspondents to live in camp and report on the boys' performance. Often the soldiers sent their own letters to the editor to local newspapers. Some couldn't spell, but most could write very well indeed after only a few years in Indiana's one-room schoolhouses. Schooling was more demanding then in many ways.

The Fourteenth was known as a "war horse" regiment—often sent into battles first to lead the troops because its soldiers were brave and didn't run. "Stick to a job till it's done. It's the way we were brought up in Indianny," the soldiers often said. But the price was very high—half of the thousand men of the Fourteenth were killed or wounded by the time the war was over. They

Civil War soldiers usually posed quite stiffly when photographed. This image of the Fourteenth Indiana was taken just after the Battle of Gettysburg. Perhaps they were so relaxed because of a renewed confidence that they would win the war after all.

stayed in what was known as the "Eastern Theater" of the war until 1864, near the end of war and were forever known after that as one of the best regiments the North produced.

—Nancy Niblack Baxter

Nineteenth Indiana Volunteers

In the summer of 1862, the expanding Union Army was joined by many eager Hoosiers. Humble men and boys from farms, villages and Hoosier cities first assembled in the nearest town—places like Goshen, Elkhart, and Muncie—to form companies and then traveled to Indianapolis where the companies merged into regiments. Formed on July 29, 1861, the Nineteenth Indiana Volunteer Infantry was filled with and led by men with little military experience; but hard work and a fierce loyalty to the Union paid off. They became members of the most famous brigade in the Civil War—the Iron Brigade, and earned glory for themselves and their state.

The regiment had a discouraging start, seeing little action for much of its first year; however, this did not mean the men were without troubles. In September and October alone, more than sixty men died from the dreaded ty-

Oliver P. Morton (1823–1877) was Indiana's governor during the Civil War. (Indiana Historical Society)

phoid fever. In the Civil War, more men died of disease than from wounds. The boring chores of camp life—drawing water, cooking, digging pits for toilets, drilling, and endless forced marches that got them nowhere—left the Hoosiers tired and eager for some real action.

This action came swiftly and brutally in August of 1862 when the Nineteenth Indiana faced Stonewall Jackson's corps of Confederate soldiers in Virginia at the Battle of Brawner Farm. Outnumbered three to one, the Union soldiers fought bravely in a deadly shootout that lasted only an hour and twenty minutes. When darkness made further fighting impossible, the Nineteenth Indiana had lost over 50 percent of its men to casualties.

The Nineteenth Indiana went on to fight in some of the most famous battles in the Civil War, including the Battle of Antietam on September 17, 1862. Considered the bloodiest one-day battle of the war, the Hoosiers again lost half of their men to the fighting. The men also participated in the Chancellorsville Campaign and at Gettysburg, where Robert E. Lee and his Confederate soldiers marched north into Pennsylvania. Again fighting bravely but in vain, the Nineteenth Indiana watched over half their troops fall to Confederate soldiers for the third time. Hardly anyone was left. In May of 1864, the Hoosiers began fighting under the leadership of Lt. General Ulysses S. Grant, who warned the men

that their days of retreating from the Rebels were over. The Nineteenth Indiana fought from June until October, 1864, cutting off food and supplies to the Confederate capital, finally allowing the Hoosiers to dominate the Confederacy and the Civil War.

—Craig Dunn

Twentieth Indiana Volunteers

When the war drums of the Civil War began beating in the spring of 1861, William Lyon Brown of Lafayette began traveling throughout central and northern Indiana trying to raise the one thousand men that he would need to form the infantry regiment he had been authorized to establish by the governor. There was no draft in America at that time; almost all the soldiers in the Civil War were volunteers. Finding the competition tough for able-bodied enlistees, Brown resorted to wild promises of granting land and gold to those who would volunteer for service. Eventually, Brown was able to gather more than a thousand men for the Twentieth Indiana Volunteers. They came from such places as Logansport, Valparaiso, Monticello, Crown Point, Plymouth, Culver, and Lafayette.

One of the regiment's early assignments was at the primitive northern end of Hatteras Island in North Carolina. On their way, the men witnessed the launching of a manned observation balloon from the decks of the *Fanny*, making them present at the origin of the first aircraft carrier. Arriving at camp a day ahead of their supplies which followed them on the *Fanny*, the men were horrified to see their ship captured only three hundred feet from shore. Without supplies, the men soon found themselves hemmed in on two sides and were forced to destroy their camp and desperately struggle for safety. Many of the Indiana men were killed and captured during the horrible escape down Hatteras Island.

The Hoosiers went to Fort Clark in order to regroup and reequip; however as soon as things began to return to normal, the men were shocked by events again out of their control. A late-season hurricane roared across the island, nearly drowning the entire regiment. All the clothing and equipment the men had been able to acquire since their escape had been washed away. Fortunately, the men were shortly returned to Virginia, where they were rearmed and reclothed.

After an uneventful winter, the men were back into the thick of battle by the first week of March, 1862. It was then that the Hoosiers, from the shore-line of Hampton Roads, battled with the famous Confederate ironclad, the USS *Virginia*, better known as the *Merrimac*. By shooting at boarding crews and any visible Rebel soldiers on deck, the men of the Twentieth Indiana were able to prevent capture of the Union's USS *Congress*. One young Hoosier wounded the *Merrimac*'s commander, preventing him from commanding in the next day's revolutionary naval battle between the *Merrimac* and the Union's ironclad, the *Monitor*.

The men of the Twentieth also participated in such battles as the Seven Days Battles, the Second Manassas Campaign, the Chancellorsville Campaign, and Gettysburg—where the men fired over 160 rounds per man and were eventually reduced to throwing rocks in order to greatly delay Rebel advances. At the Battle of Wilderness, under the command of Ulysses S. Grant, the men saved the Union Army from certain destruction with a well-timed counterattack.

The Twentieth Indiana moved with the Army of Potomac in June, 1864 to Petersburg, where they dug trenches and bomb-proof shelters, a preview of war tactics to come during World War I. These Hoosiers of the Twentieth Indiana were soon to fight in the final Appomattox Campaign and witness the surrender of Robert E. Lee's army.

— Craig Dunn

Read more about the Nineteenth Indiana and the famous Twentieth Indiana in Craig Dunn's books, Iron Men, Iron Will *and* Harvestfields of Death, *both from Guild Press of Indiana.*

A soldier's letter home

Strausburg, Va. March 28th [1862]

Dear Sister

I once more have the pleasure of seating my self to answer your most welcome letter which I received not long since. I expect you folks has been some what uneasy since the battle we had at Winchester but I can assure you that I am all right yet, there was not a bullet grazed by my hide. Henderson got a slight wound in the arm. It will not be long before he will be well. It is of no use for me to tell you any thing about the fight because you can read it in he papers only I can tell you that the 14th done her best. The 13th Ind fought by the side of us all yelling like Indians, there was only four hurt in our company. John Conly got his left fore finger shot off. Mike Murville slightly wounded in the leg. Tom Bailey just tipped the side of his head, it knocked him down but he jumped up after the secesh again. I don't know whether this letter will get to you or not. They have been talking about not letting letters home for 30 days. Henderson did not get to shoot but three shots. I will have to come to a close it is about bed time and I will write again soon.

Yours Truly, John R. McClure

You can read more about John McClure in the book Hoosier Farmboy in Lincoln's Army *by Nancy Niblack Baxter.*

Benjamin and Caroline Harrison

More than one president of the United States has had a Hoosier connection.

William Henry Harrison, the president in 1841, was governor of the Indiana Territory earlier in his life. **Abraham Lincoln** grew up in Indiana, living here from ages seven to twenty-one. (See profiles of these distinguished men earlier in this book.) At the point in their careers when they were elected to our nation's highest office, though, William Henry Harrison and Lincoln were living in neighboring states—"Ol' Tippecanoe" Harrison in Ohio, and "Honest Abe" Lincoln in Illinois.

Only one president and first lady were living in Indiana when the American people voted them into the White House: Indianapolis resident **Benjamin Harrison** and his wife, **Caroline Scott Harrison**.

Benjamin Harrison (1833–1901), a Republican, was the nation's twenty-third chief executive (serving as president from 1888–1892), and was William Henry's grandson. The younger Harrison's elegant home on North Delaware Street near Downtown Indianapolis—where Benjamin Harrison lived both before and after his White House days—is open for visitors and fascinating to tour. It's particularly spectacular during the holiday season because the Harrisons were the first residents of the White House to have a decorated Christmas tree. (Before the 1880s, people didn't tend to put ornaments and glitter on Christmas trees.)

The Harrisons also were the first presidential pair to have the new invention of electricity in the White House. In fact, there was a worker at the White House whose job was to follow around the "first family"—Benjamin, Caroline, their children, and their grandchildren, many of whom lived with them—and flick on the light switches in each room. This way, the worker (not the family members) would get "shocked" by the burst of crude electricity.

Other "firsts" also occurred during the Harrisons' stay in the White House. Caroline Scott Harrison (1832–1892), a gentle woman who loved to paint with watercolors and grow orchids, started the White House's famous collection of china—plates, bowls, teacups, and saucers. To this day, if you tour the White House, you will find the official painting of Caroline Scott Harrison hanging on a wall near the china collection as a tribute to this gracious woman.

While not considered among the

This portrait of Caroline Scott Harrison hangs in the White House near the China Room as a tribute because she started the china collection. (Indiana Historical Society)

This group of Hoosiers called itself "Benjie's Ducking Club." It was a hunting group of Benjamin Harrison and his friends; they are shown here on an outing in 1891. (Indiana Historical Society)

Benjamin and Caroline Harrison at an Army-Navy reception at the White House during his presidency. (Indiana Historical Society)

greatest American presidents, Benjamin Harrison achieved several distinctions in the White House. He became known as "the Centennial (one hundred-year) President" because he was elected almost a hundred years after George Washington, our first president. So Benjamin Harrison presided over celebrations in Washington, D.C., and across the country.

He was challenged by some severe economic (money) problems in the country during his stay in the White House. But Harrison was commended for cutting ties to many Republican "bosses" in big cities—although that hurt him in terms of politics.

"When I came to power," Harrison said later, "I found that the party managers had taken it all to themselves."

Harrison also was commended for overseeing a historic law in 1890. Called the Sherman Anti-trust Act, it helped prevent the buildup of a single big business (or monopoly) in various industries. Monopolies had been killing small businesses across the country.

Who were Benjamin and Caroline Scott Harrison in private life?

Both were born in Ohio. Benjamin Harrison grew up on a family farm; his father, John Harrison, was William Henry's son. Caroline's father was a science teacher at a college in Ohio. Known as Farmers College, it was near where Benjamin was studying law. The Harrisons married in 1853.

The next year, they moved to Indianapolis. Benjamin had concluded the capital of Indiana offered great opportunities for a young lawyer.

A very private person and devoted family man, Benjamin Harrison wore a beard almost his entire life—both when it was in and out of style. He became a very successful courtroom lawyer and a doting father. The Harrisons had two children—a son, Russell, and a daughter, Mary. Both were born in the 1850s.

During the 1860s, Harrison was called to duty in the Civil War. At the request of the governor of Indiana, Harrison raised a group of fighting men known as the Seventeenth Indiana Regiment. He trained the Hoosier men, and then became a brave leader in battles in the South, including a conflict known as the Peachtree Creek battle in Georgia.

By the end of the Civil War, Harrison was a top-ranking general and was considered a war hero. All of that helped him win election as U.S. senator from Indiana in 1881. In the Senate, Harrison was known as "the soldier's friend" because he fought for ways to help fellow Civil War veterans. With that kind of reputation, Harrison beat Grover Cleveland, the Democrat, in the race for president in 1888.

It was an entirely different story four years later in 1892, which was a deeply painful year in several ways for Benjamin Harrison.

In an unusual twist, Cleveland came back from defeat and beat Harrison in their second race for the White House. Harrison didn't even

Fun facts about the Harrisons

- When the Harrisons lived in the White House, there was a goat on the property. The goat's name was "His Whiskers." He was the pet of Benjamin and Caroline Harrisons' grandchildren, who lived in the White House with the president and first lady. The goat didn't roam the hallways of the White House, though. He was kept in the White House stable with the horses.

- Devoted to work and his family, Benjamin Harrison had very few hobbies. But he loved to smoke cigars and to go duck hunting.

- Benjamin Harrison was our second-shortest president. Sometimes nicknamed "Little Ben," he stood between five feet, six inches and five feet, seven inches tall. Only our fourth president, James Madison of Virginia, was shorter.

- Caroline Scott Harrison was the second first lady to die in the White House. (The first was the wife of John Tyler, who was president in the 1840s.)

campaign across the country because of a tragic personal situation: Caroline Scott Harrison was ill and dying in the White House.

She suffered from tuberculosis, a disease that affects breathing and killed thousands of Americans every year in the late 1800s. With Caroline so ill, the Harrisons' daughter, Mary, substituted for her mother at White House events—and Harrison announced that he would not leave his wife's side in Washington, D.C., to go on the campaign trail.

Caroline Scott Harrison died two weeks before her husband lost his second presidential race. Thousands of Indianapolis residents watched her funeral procession to Crown Hill Cemetery.

Sad and lonely, Harrison returned to his house on North Delaware Street. There, he picked up his career as a lawyer—and won more rave reviews for his talent in the courtroom.

Eventually, he married again. Harrison and his second wife, Mary, even had a child. Their daughter, Elizabeth, was born when her father was sixty-three years old.

She was just four years old when Benjamin Harrison died in 1901.

May Wright Sewall

In the 1800s and early 1900s, women could not vote. During this era, many Americans assumed that women did not have the intelligence or insight of men. Even the physical development of girls was not considered important, or especially desirable; it was almost unheard of for girls' schools and academies to have a gymnasium. Classes at even the best academies for girls often were not nearly as challenging as the courses for boys.

In Indianapolis, a colorful, energetic woman was determined to change all of that. May Wright Sewall often was called "the leader of 500,000 women" because of her key role in so many women's organizations across the country—and her speeches around the world. She made her mark in half a dozen fields—from teacher and peace activist to suffragette (or, as she preferred, suffragist), a person who advocates extending the right to vote to all adults.

"My country is the world," May Wright Sewall announced. "My countrymen are all mankind."

That was one of her favorite sayings. Rest assured that when she spoke of "countrymen" and "mankind," May certainly was including women and girls. She spent her life crusading

May Wright Sewall, a famous suffragist, teacher and civic leader. (Courtesy of the Propylaeum Club)

on their behalf. But May's ideas were considered so radical that she often had to meet with her friends and followers in secret.

Who was this remarkable woman who became one of the best-known Hoosiers of the early 1900s?

When she was born in Wisconsin in 1844, her name was May Elizabeth Wright. A bright child, she was reading classical works such as *The Odyssey* by age seven. Her father, a teacher who became a farmer, encouraged May to enrich her mind and to attend college at a time when few women did so.

May became a teacher of English and German. She taught in schools as far away as Mississippi and Michigan. When she married her first husband, Edwin Thompson, the couple moved to Indianapolis in 1874. Both had been hired to teach at Indianapolis High School. (It later became Shortridge High School.)

Just one year after he and May moved, Edwin Thompson died of tuberculosis. May joined the faculty at the prestigious Indianapolis Classical School for Boys, an elite private school. Its founder, Theodore Sewall, became May's second husband.

In 1882, she persuaded Theodore to open the Classical School for Girls. The couple ran both schools; at May's insistence, the classes were identical, with an emphasis on Latin, Greek and the classics of world literature. The girls' school even had a gymnasium!

May took pride in hiring all of the teachers personally.

The Classical School for Girls was only one of her interests, though. In 1875, she helped form the Indianapolis Woman's Club. She also was a founder of an arts association that later became the Indianapolis Museum of Art.

Also in the 1870s, May began bringing together Hoosier women with "advanced ideas" about working for equal rights. The women—many of them wives of Indianapolis's most prominent men—met in secret to form the Equal Suffrage Society of Indianapolis. To many people, the thought of women voting for president, mayor and other public officials was laughable—or dangerous. A woman's sphere—or place—was in the home!

That didn't stop May, who challenged old ways in almost every aspect of life. A stocky, sensible woman, she was one of the first women in Indianapolis to wear her skirts at ankle length—a shocking move in an era when women's skirts swept the ground. In 1890 she realized one of her dreams with the opening of the Indianapolis Propylaeum, a club and building managed by women for women. (The Propylaeum is still thriving in a historic home on North Delaware Street.)

To May's relief, her activism didn't create problems at home. Theodore Sewall took pride in his wife's successes. She was devastated when

Theodore, like her first husband, died of tuberculosis in 1895.

Despite her grief, May kept crusading. In the 1890s, she went national. She founded the International Council of Women and served as president of several other large, influential women's groups. To rally women and speak about world peace, she traveled throughout Europe.

Her health began to fail, though. Sadly, the leader who spent her life advancing the causes of women never got the chance to cast a ballot in an American presidential election. May Wright Sewall died in Indianapolis in 1920, a few months before women voted in national elections for the first time.

"What she wrought will endure," another Hoosier suffragist said of May. "Generations yet unborn will find life a fuller and richer experience because she joined in the effort to make it so instead of supinely accepting conditions as they were."

Read more about May Wright Sewall in But I Do Clamor *by Ray Boomhower (Guild Press of Indiana).*

Eugene V. Debs

Eugene V. Debs, labor organizer. (Indiana Historical Society)

It's strange but true: There once was a man who ran for president of the United States while he was in jail.

Eugene V. Debs (1855–1926) of Terre Haute campaigned for president five times, always as the candidate of a third party—that is, not the Democratic or Republican parties. He was the candidate of the Socialist Party. Debs received his most votes—more than nine hundred thousand—in the 1920 presidential race, which occurred while he was in a federal prison.

In fact, his campaign played up the fact that he was a prison inmate. Campaign buttons featured his convict number (9653) and a picture of his face behind bars.

Why was Debs in prison at age sixty-five? He was a pacifist—that is, he did not believe in waging war. So he was jailed under a special law during World War I (1914–1918) that prohibited Americans from speaking out against the war. Warren G. Harding, the Republican Party candidate who defeated Debs in that 1920 election, freed him from jail on Christmas Day of 1921—in part because Debs by then was elderly and ill.

Debs was famous for a lot more than his unusual campaigns for president. He founded the Socialist Party in the United States and organized labor unions (groups of working men and women) across the country.

In the early 1900s, the average person's workday was twelve hours long. (Today, the typical workday lasts eight hours.) On top of that, many Americans worked six days each week. Debs crusaded for shorter workdays and shorter workweeks. He also fought for sick leave and more opportunities for women.

Although many of Debs' ideas were considered radical during his lifetime, several of them have become standard business practices in the decades since he died.

Did you know?

- Many legendary Hoosiers considered Eugene V. Debs a close friend, even though they disagreed with his politics. James Whitcomb Riley even praised Debs in a poem about Terre Haute. The two famous Hoosiers were such buddies that a bedroom in Debs' home is still known as "The Riley Room" because the poet stayed there so often while visiting Debs and his wife, Katherine. (The historic house where the Debses lived is open for tours; it is located near the campus of Indiana State University.)

- Debs' father immigrated to America from France. He owned a general store in Terre Haute. Eugene, who was one of ten children in the family, quit school at age fourteen to go to work for the railroad.

- His hands were badly gnarled for most of his adult life. According to some accounts, one of Debs' many jobs was to blame. He worked as a sign painter. The harsh chemicals that were used to make and strip paint in the late 1800s may have damaged his hands.

- Debs' most famous quotation is: "While there is a lower class, I am in it; while there is a criminal element, I am of it; while there is a soul in prison, I am not free!"

Madam C. J. Walker

The life of **Madam C. J. Walker** is one of the most remarkable success stories in American (not just Indiana) history. She was born to former slaves on a cotton plantation in the South, was orphaned, then became a single parent who washed clothes for a living. Yet she ended up as probably the nation's first black woman millionaire, or close to it. Madam Walker made most of her fortune—and provided thousands of jobs—in **Indianapolis**. She also was a pioneer in race relations and the advancement of women in the business world.

"I got myself a start by giving myself a start," Madam Walker said in 1917.

The entrepreneur who would become famous as "Madam Walker" in the hair care business was named Sarah Breedlove when she was born in 1867 on a cotton plantation near Delta, Louisiana. Life on the plantation, called Grand View, was rough. Sarah's parents, Owen and Minerva Breedlove, were sharecroppers—that is, they worked in the fields, but didn't own the land or the crops. They died when Sarah was six or seven years old.

Sarah tried to work in the fields, but she was too small and young. To make matters worse, the cotton crop failed and an epidemic of yellow fever struck

Madam C. J. Walker gave money to help the YMCA and many other community organizations. This photo was taken in July 1913 at the dedication of the Senate Avenue YMCA in Indianapolis. (Indiana Historical Society)

Did you know?

- Madam Walker's great-great-granddaughter, A'Lelia Bundles, has written a children's book about her famous relative. The biography is titled *Madam C. J. Walker* (Chelsea House Publishers, 1991), It's part of the "Black Americans of Achievement" series.

- During her years in Indianapolis, Madam Walker was a major community leader in addition to being a successful businesswoman. She gave thousands of dollars to YMCAs, YWCAs, and to a home for the elderly.

- Madam Walker stood up to prejudice—both because she was black and because she was a woman. At a national convention of black business leaders in 1912, she was denied a request to speak from the stage. So on the last day of the convention, she rose up and said, "I am a woman who came from the cotton fields of the South . . . I was promoted from there to the washtub. Then I was promoted to the cook kitchen, and from there I promoted myself into the business of manufacturing hair goods . . . I have built my own factory on my own ground." Her speech was such a hit that she was invited back the next year as the keynote (main) speaker.

in 1878. So Sarah, now ten years old, moved with an older sister, Louvenia, to Vicksburg, Mississippi. To support themselves, the girls took in laundry and worked as servants for white families. At the time, laundry work was almost as backbreaking as share-cropping: Dirty clothes were washed in large tubs, scrubbed on washboards, and beaten with sticks.

At fourteen, Sarah married a Vicks-burg resident named Moses McWilliams. Three years later in 1885—at age seventeen—she gave birth to their daughter, Lelia. (Lelia would later become her mother's business partner under the name A'Lelia Walker.) Lelia was just two years old when her father was killed in an accident.

What was Sarah, a twenty-year-old widow and single mother, to do?

She dreamed of a better life in the North for herself and her daughter. Sarah had been told that wages were higher in St. Louis than in Mississippi, so she headed north. For the next seventeen years, she struggled to make a living as a laundress.

When a horrified Sarah noticed that some of her hair was falling out, her life changed. She was suffering from an ailment common among black women then because of poor diet, damaging hair-care treatments, and stress. Sarah decided to develop her own line of hair care products.

In July 1905, with only a dollar and a half in savings, Sarah and Lelia moved to Denver. Sarah began selling her hair-care products door-to-door, and married a salesman named Charles Joseph Walker.

Now known as Madam C. J. Walker, she developed shampoos, hair medications, and combs. She opened a mail-order business, a beauty parlor, and a training school.

Her move to Indianapolis in 1910 was a business decision. The Hoosier capital then was one of the country's largest manufacturing centers. With eight major railways in the area, it was easy for Madam Walker to ship her products all over the country.

Madam Walker hired former maids, housewives, schoolteachers, and farm workers. Eventually, she employed more than twenty thousand people in jobs ranging from factory worker to sales agent.

In 1916, she moved to New York City and asked three staff members to manage her Indianapolis operations. Madam Walker lived on the East Coast for only three years before she died in 1919. By then, she was considered the wealthiest black woman in America.

Upon her death, she was followed as company president by A'Lelia—once the little girl for whom Madam Walker had sacrificed so much.

A look at the Walker Center

Near the end of her life, Madam Walker began planning details of a magnificent building on Indiana Avenue in Indianapolis. It wasn't until 1927, eight years after her death, that the four-story Walker Building opened. In addition to being the world headquarters of the Walker family's manufacturing business, the Walker Building housed popular restaurants (one was called the Walker Coffee Pot), a drugstore, a ballroom, and a beauty college.

In the 1940s and '50s, the triangle-shaped Walker Building became the hub of bustling Indiana Avenue. The avenue, in turn, became the center of African-American music and business life in Indianapolis. So on top of everything else, the Walker Building served as a symbol of ethnic pride.

During the 1970s, however, businesses moved elsewhere, and the Walker Building deteriorated. It was saved from demolition, then got a glorious new life. After a massive renovation, the building reopened in 1988 as the Madame Walker Urban Life Center. The stunning building includes a majestic theater that seats 950 people; the Walker Theatre has elaborate carvings celebrating African folklore and culture. The center also includes a room known as the Madam C. J. Walker Memorial Room. (Photo by Stephen Baker)

D. C. Stephenson

A legendary Hoosier of the 1920s was one of the most despicable men in Indiana history. D. C. Stephenson, the leader of a notorious group called the Ku Klux Klan, is included in this book because to overlook him would be to ignore a shameful part of the state's past. It was an era when, unfortunately, Stephenson enjoyed enormous power across Indiana.

D. C. Stephenson (1891–1966) held the title of "Grand Dragon" as the Midwest leader of the Ku Klux Klan, or KKK. Group members met—and continue to meet—in secret. They hide their faces behind white hoods and sheets as they try to drum up resentment against people whom they consider "different"—particularly black people, Catholics, Jews, and foreigners.

When Stephenson was running the KKK during the 1920s, the racist group claimed a membership of about a quarter of a million people in Indiana. The Klan took credit for electing a governor and openly controlled an Indianapolis mayor.

Thankfully, Stephenson's reign was brief. His downfall was just as spectacular as his rise to power. He was arrested after the tragic death in 1925 of Madge Oberholtzer, one of his neighbors in the Irvington area on the east side of Indianapolis. Stephenson

The notorious D. C. Stephenson, leader of the Ku Klux Klan. (Courtesy of *The Indianapolis Star*)

After the Stephenson trial

- In 1928, *The Indianapolis Times* won a Pulitzer Prize, journalism's highest honor, for its investigations of the Klan in Indiana.

- John Niblack eventually became a judge, serving on Marion County's Circuit Court bench.

- Will Remy went on to head up the city of Indianapolis' safety board, which oversaw the police.

- Asa Smith served his country in war for a second time: He was a Marine during World War II. After returning to Indiana, Asa Smith conducted investigations in yet another scandal: Several officials of the State Highway Department were convicted of taking bribes in the 1950s, and Asa Smith helped gather the evidence.

served thirty-one years at the Indiana State Prison after being convicted of second-degree murder in Oberholtzer's death.

How did such a hateful man ever gain power in the first place?

Stephenson was a smooth talker—and, as his biographer put it, "a chronic liar." He was born in Texas and dropped out of school after the eighth grade. After he drifted to Evansville in 1920, Stephenson falsely claimed to have been successful in several professions, including the law. Actually, he had struggled at several low-paying jobs and had abandoned a wife and daughter in Oklahoma.

His arrival in Indiana occurred at the same time that the KKK was stepping up its efforts to recruit members in the North. The group had maintained a strong presence in some Southern states since the Civil War. The Klan sensed opportunities in Indiana because of a backlash against foreigners following World War I (1914–1918).

A powerful speaker, Stephenson turned out to be an effective recruiter. Nearly 30 percent of Indiana's white, native-born men joined up. Stephenson became wealthy because he enjoyed a cut on sales of new Klan memberships and sales of KKK sheets and hoods.

At one point, Stephenson and his cronies convinced the mayor of Indianapolis and the Marion County sheriff to sign pledges saying they only would appoint people to top jobs who were acceptable to Stephenson.

"I am the law in Indiana," Stephenson declared.

His power was shattered by the scandal involving Madge Oberholtzer. She died after swallowing poison—and blamed Stephenson on her deathbed, saying he had attacked her during a train ride.

After Stephenson's downfall, the Klan lost most of its influence on Indiana politicians. KKK membership rapidly declined, and most Hoosiers were ashamed they had let the state fall into the hands of hooded thugs.

The Hoosiers who brought Stephenson down

In the scandalous trial of Ku Klux Klan leader D. C. Stephenson, the case against him was handled by a youthful-looking "boy prosecutor" and a hard-working lawyer who had been a war hero. Those two men, along with a newspaper reporter, are credited with toppling the KKK in Indiana.

The former war hero was Asa Smith (1894–1973), an Indianapolis attorney. Just thirty-one years old in 1925, Smith had fought the Germans as a Marine in World War I. His eyes had been damaged by mustard gas in battle, so he wore thick glasses for the rest of his life.

But he was bursting with zeal in the Stephenson case. Outraged by the plight of Madge Oberholtzer, he questioned her as she lay dying. The statements that Smith took from her helped build the case against Stephenson.

The prosecutor in the case was William Remy—who already had clashed with Stephenson before they faced each other in the courtroom. The KKK leader had tried to block Remy's appointment to the prosecutor job. Early in his career, Remy (1892–1968) had been invited to a meeting in the back room of a hotel along with other public officials.

There, the other officials promised to support Stephenson—but Remy declined, which infuriated Stephenson.

Stephenson's trial was held in Hamilton County. Reporters who squeezed into the packed courtroom referred to Remy as the "boy prosecutor" because he looked so young—even though he was a few years older than Asa Smith. To wrap up his case against the KKK leader, Will Remy delivered a stirring, three-hour speech to the all-male jury.

"He said he was the law in Indiana," Remy reminded them. "And gentlemen . . . Thank God he can't say he was the law in Hamilton County."

After that, the jury convicted Stephenson. By then, public opinion across Indiana already was turning against the KKK—thanks in many ways to a series of articles in *The Indianapolis Times* newspaper. Reporters, including John Niblack (1897–1986), exposed many activities of the racist group. After that, Niblack became a deputy prosecutor. He assisted in trials against several of the politicians who were connected with the Klan; they were brought up on charges of bribery and corrupt practices.

John Dillinger

Americans sometimes have glamorized criminals, lawbreakers, and celebrities who misbehave. We turn the wrong people into role models. Such was the case with John Dillinger of Mooresville, who became famous during the Depression of the 1930s for the wrong reasons.

To some people, John Dillinger (1903–1934) was a folk hero. But he really was a bank robber—and he was dangerous. Law enforcement officials considered him Public Enemy Number One. Even though Dillinger was compared to Robin Hood, there was a big, important difference between the Indiana farm boy gone wrong and the fictional Robin Hood of the English woods. Dillinger didn't rob from the rich and give to the poor; he kept the stolen money for himself!

Keep in mind that many Americans, including thousands of Hoosiers, did not admire Dillinger, who robbed banks across the state of Indiana. It's said that locksmiths made fortunes because Dillinger, who twice escaped from jail, frightened many Hoosiers into making their homes safer and more secure.

For eighteen months in 1933–1934, Dillinger was at the top of the federal government's "Most Wanted" list. While he was in hiding, Dillinger did

This was the "wanted poster" for John Dillinger in 1934, when federal agents considered him "Public Enemy Number One." Dillinger later scarred off his fingerprints by dipping his hands in acid. (Indiana Historical Society)

many things to change his appearance—including wearing eyeglasses, dying his hair darker and undergoing plastic surgery on his face in East Chicago, Indiana.

Dillinger almost died during the surgery because it was performed by a criminal doctor in a house, not a hospital. Of course, no honest doctor would operate on an outlaw like Dillinger. (A few weeks later, Dillinger went back to the doctor's home for another "operation": he stuck his hands in acid. Dillinger wanted to scar off his fingerprints so the police would not find him.)

In the end, nothing helped. Dillinger died at age thirty-one in a dark alley near the Biograph movie theater in Chicago. He was killed in a shootout with federal agents. They had been given a "hot tip" that Dillinger would be seeing a movie in the theater.

Milestones in the life of the gangster:

- 1903—John Dillinger is born in Indianapolis. His father is a grocer. His mother dies when John is three years old.

- 1919—At age sixteen, John quits school. The Dillingers move to a sixty-acre farm near Mooresville. Young John tells his buddies that he idolizes Wild West gunslinger Jesse James.

- 1924—Dillinger pals around with an older ex-convict. The two are arrested after they rob and beat an elderly man who owns a grocery store. Dillinger is sent to prison.

- 1933—Released from prison, he kicks off his bank-robbing crime spree during the Depression. With families and businesses struggling because many Americans are out of work, banks are forced to shut down and give people back only part of their money. For that reason, some people applaud Dillinger for robbing banks.

- 1934—Hiding in Chicago, Dillinger is betrayed by a lady friend named Anna Sage. She is a friend and landlady of Dillinger's girlfriend. Anna Sage becomes known in folklore as "The Lady in Red" —although Anna Sage said later that she actually was wearing an orange skirt. Anna Sage tells authorities that she, Dillinger and his girlfriend will attend a movie at the Biograph Theatre in Chicago. A special squad of courageous Federal agents, headed by agent Melvin Purvis, has been tracking Dillinger. They trap the gangster as he exits the theater. As Dillinger reaches for his gun, he is shot to death.

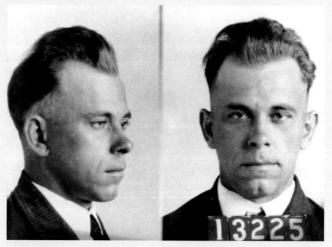

These were young John Dillinger's prison photos in Pendleton, Indiana. (Indiana State Archives)

Herman B Wells

He was nicknamed "Mr. IU." That's because Herman B Wells—who looked a little like Santa Claus without a beard—was the major figure on the Bloomington campus of Indiana University for more than eighty years.

Also just like Santa Claus, Herman B Wells (1902–2000) had a jolly personality and was widely loved. But he also was extremely clever and imaginative—"brilliant," many people said—as well as courageous. His achievements include helping make the IU School of Music and the School of Business among the most respected music and business schools in the country.

He also stood up to IU fans who did not want coaches to recruit black athletes. During the twenty-five years that Wells served as IU president (1938–1962), an outstanding high school athlete from Shelbyville named Bill Garrett became the first black player on a Big Ten basketball team. (The Big Ten is a group of large colleges in the Midwest; it includes IU, Purdue, the University of Michigan and Ohio State University.)

Wells never bragged about his leadership.

"My role has been greatly exaggerated," or "You'll have to talk to

Herman B Wells, "Mr. IU" (Courtesy of *The Indianapolis Star*)

someone else about that," he used to say when people asked him about his accomplishments at IU.

Herman B Wells first showed up on campus in the early 1920s as a fun-loving, teenage student. He never really moved away from Bloomington. For nearly forty-five years—from 1962 to his death in 2000—he was the university chancellor, a top post at a college.

He was born in a small cottage in tiny Jamestown in Boone County. The whole town only had six hundred people then; his family's cottage didn't even have electricity or an indoor bathroom. Yet he ended up, because of his glory at IU, getting to meet the queen of England and other world leaders.

Among Wells' talents was the ability to hire excellent, dedicated teachers.

"He always took great care," said Frank Banta, a retired IU professor of German. "He chose outstanding faculty, gave people support when they needed it, and otherwise kept out of their way."

Herman B Wells was ninety-seven years old when he died. He never married or had children. But to thousands of IU graduates, he was a father figure.

Fun facts

- There is no period after the "B" in Herman B Wells. That's because his parents couldn't agree on a middle name, but they wanted one that began with "B." (Middle names with "B" were a family custom.) So the letter "B" stood alone in his name.

- Both of Wells' parents were teachers. His father also was a farmer and later became a banker in Lebanon. Young Herman began life in the tiny cottage in Jamestown, then moved to a ten-acre farm with chickens and pigs. (Unlike their cottage, the family's farmhouse, thankfully, had electricity.) When Herman was in high school, the family moved to the city of Lebanon.

- Herman B Wells had many passions, or loves. He loved opera and classical music. He loved to eat. He loved to read. And he loved to talk to young people. If you visit Indiana University, look for a life-sized sculpture of Herman B Wells on campus. The sculpture is seated on a park bench and has its right hand extended as if greeting a new student—just as Herman B Wells did so often.

Dan Quayle

Dan Quayle, vice president from 1988 to 1992. (Courtesy of the office of former U.S. Vice President Dan Quayle)

Marilyn Quayle, attorney and former "second lady." (Courtesy of *The Indianapolis Star*)

So far, only one person—Benjamin Harrison of Indianapolis—has been elected president of the United States while living in Indiana. But five politicians from Indiana have served as vice president. That's a large number for a medium-sized state, and it's the reason that Indiana sometimes is called the "mother of vice presidents."

More vice presidents (three of them) are buried in beautiful Crown Hill Cemetery in Indianapolis than in any other graveyard in the country.

Dan Quayle (1947–), who grew up in **Huntington**, was just forty-one years old in August of 1988 when George Bush Sr. picked the Republican from Indiana as his running mate. Quayle served as vice president for four years (1988–1992). Before that, Dan Quayle—whose full name is James Danforth Quayle—was a U.S. senator from Indiana.

When he won his first race for the Senate in 1980, Quayle was only thirty-three years old—which made him the youngest senator ever elected from Indiana. His youth, good looks, enthusiasm and emphasis on family values made Quayle a popular figure among many Americans, particularly people who are politically conservative. Other people, though, poked fun at what they considered to be Quayle's lack of intelligence and experience.

Comedians and talk show hosts—including fellow Hoosier David Letterman—often made "Dan Quayle jokes."

"I laughed at the jokes that were funny and ignored the others," Quayle said in an interview in 1997. "My kids did the same thing."

Quayle and his wife, **Marilyn Tucker Quayle** (1949–), who grew up in Indianapolis, have three children: Tucker, Benjamin, and Corinne.

Both of the Quayles are attorneys. For a few years in the 1970s, they also ran *The Huntington Herald-Press*, the newspaper in Dan Quayle's hometown. (Quayle's father had owned the paper when Dan was growing up.)

In the U.S. Senate, Quayle's proudest achievement was the Job Training and Partnership Act of 1982. As vice president, he hoped to serve eight years, not just four. But in 1992, the team of George Bush Sr. and Dan Quayle was defeated for re-election by the Democratic ticket of Bill Clinton and Al Gore.

Since the mid-1990s, the Quayles have lived primarily in Arizona. Marilyn has become an author. She has written two thriller novels: *Embrace the Serpent* (1992) and *The Campaign* (1996). As the country's "second lady" when Quayle was vice president, Marilyn made disaster relief her major focus and frequently traveled across the country with American Red Cross workers to help victims of floods, tornadoes and hurricanes.

The other vice presidents from Indiana

Schuyler Colfax

Schuyler Colfax was the first Hoosier to become vice president of the United States. Colfax was a Republican from South Bend who served as vice president from 1868–1872, when Civil War hero Ulysses S. Grant was president. Colfax (1823–1885) attended school only until he was ten years old; he quit to work as a store clerk and help support his family.

Before becoming vice president, he was a U.S. congressman. In the final years of his life, Colfax—who was nicknamed "The Smiler"—became a popular public speaker.

Thomas A. Hendricks

A farm in Shelby County was the birthplace of this vice president, who served for only eight months: March to November in 1885. Thomas Hendricks (1819–1885), a Democrat, died at his home in Indianapolis. A former U.S. senator from Indiana, Hendricks had suffered strokes that left him partially paralyzed and able to see out of only one eye. He is buried in Crown Hill Cemetery.

Charles W. Fairbanks

Charles Fairbanks was born in Ohio in a one-room log cabin, but moved to Indianapolis in the 1870s to work as a lawyer. Fairbanks (1852–1918) was such a successful attorney that he became wealthy, eventually owning *The Indianapolis News*. A Republican, he served as vice president from 1905 to 1909 under President Theodore Roosevelt.

Thomas R. Marshall

The saying, "What this country needs is a good five-cent cigar," began with one of Indiana's vice presidents.

It was one of many popular quips made by Thomas R. Marshall (1854–1925), a lawyer from Columbia City. A Democrat, he attended Wabash College. Marshall served as vice president (1913–1921) during World War I under President Woodrow Wilson. Another one of Marshall's famous remarks is a joke about how little attention most Americans pay to the vice president:

"Once there were two brothers. One ran away to sea, the other was elected vice president, and neither of them was heard from again."

Thomas R. Marshall
(Bass Photo Company Collection/
Indiana Historical Society)

Evan Bayh

In any national list of young stars in the Democratic Party of the late 1990s and early 2000s, the name of **Evan Bayh** almost always is included.

He was elected to the U.S. Senate in 1998, winning in a landslide. Before that, Bayh served as a popular governor of the Hoosier state for two terms (or eight years), from 1988 to 1996.

Known as the "boy governor" because of his youth, handsome Evan Bayh was thirty-two years old when he first was elected—making him the youngest governor in the country at the time. He won his second term with the largest margin of victory for any Indiana governor of the twentieth century.

In 2001, Evan Bayh became chairman of the Democratic Leadership Council, a national group of top politicians who are more moderate or conservative than others in their party. According to many reports, Bayh came close to being selected as the Democratic Party's candidate for vice president in 2000. (The presidential candidate, Bayh's friend Al Gore, lost to George W. Bush.)

Evan Bayh's personal life has intrigued the public for years. For one thing, his U.S. Senate seat once was held by his father—highly unusual in American history! Bayh (who was born

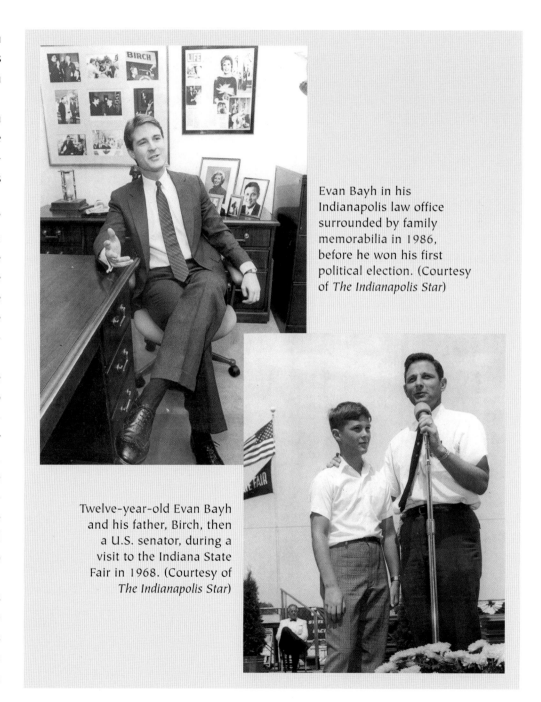

Evan Bayh in his Indianapolis law office surrounded by family memorabilia in 1986, before he won his first political election. (Courtesy of *The Indianapolis Star*)

Twelve-year-old Evan Bayh and his father, Birch, then a U.S. senator, during a visit to the Indiana State Fair in 1968. (Courtesy of *The Indianapolis Star*)

in 1955) grew up in the spotlight as a "senator's kid," the son of a distinguished U.S. senator from Indiana, Birch Bayh. (Evan's full name is Birch Evan Bayh III.)

In the 1970s, young Evan and his mother, Marvella, campaigned across the country for Birch Bayh when he ran twice for president. Both crusades for the Democratic nomination were brief and unsuccessful, but young Evan got his feet wet in politics. Even then, observers noticed Evan Bayh's manners and sense of maturity. Sometimes, he is criticized for being too stilted or formal.

"People say to me, 'No one can be polite all the time,'" Evan Bayh said in an interview. "I do have moments when I fall short. But growing up in the public eye, you always know that you are a reflection of your parents. I never wanted to let them down."

Sadly, Bayh's mother would not live to see her son's greatest successes. Marvella Bayh died of breast cancer in 1979. By then, Bayh had graduated from Indiana University. He became a lawyer and entered politics in Indianapolis.

His family life began to interest the public in other ways. In 1985, with his father serving as his best man, Bayh married a blond, vivacious lawyer; Susan Bayh quickly became a popular public figure in Indiana. (Some people joked that the attractive couple reminded them of "Ken and Barbie dolls.")

In 1995, Evan and Susan Bayh became the parents of twin sons. They are Nicholas Harrison Bayh and Birch Evan Bayh IV, known as "Beau."

The twins were shown on national TV in 1996 when Evan Bayh was chosen to give the keynote address—the kickoff speech—at the Democratic National Convention. At the time, Evan Bayh was winning praise for not raising taxes and balancing the state budget in Indiana.

While his once-famous father stepped out of the spotlight (Birch Bayh now is a private lawyer in Washington, D.C.), Evan is never far from media attention. Since winning the U.S. Senate seat once held by his dad, Evan Bayh has said many times that he simply wants to be the best possible senator from Indiana. Many others, though, predict that he will run for vice president or even president someday.

Young Hoosier Legends

Frances Slocum

The dramatic story of **Frances Slocum** has been told to generations of Hoosier boys and girls. It's been the subject of dozens of books, tributes and poems about American frontier life.

The legend about the little white girl known as Frances Slocum—who grew up to become a woman known to Native Americans as **Maconaquah** (and known in folklore as "The Lost Sister of Wyoming" and "The White Rose of the Miami")—continues to fascinate us because it shows the clash of two cultures on the frontier. They were two cultures that, tragically, could not exist with each other.

Frances' story begins on the Pennsylvania frontier—specifically, in a cabin near the lush woods of the Wyoming Valley. That's where Frances was born in 1773. On a November morning when she was five years old, Frances was barefoot and playing outdoors with her younger brother. Her father and grandfather were working in the fields, and her mother was doing housework in the cabin. Two neighbor boys were sharpening a knife near the Slocums' cabin door; one of the boys was wearing a military uniform.

This was a tense time in most frontier homes. The Revolutionary War was under way, and the Delaware

Frances Slocum was a white child who spent most of her life among Native Americans and, as an old woman, refused to leave her home with the Miami. (Indiana Historical Society)

Indians in Pennsylvania were siding with the British against the American colonists. Several colonist families in the Wyoming Valley had been killed. Other families had fled the valley in fear, taking shelter in forts in the Pennsylvania wilderness.

The Slocums felt safe, though. They were Quakers and pacifists—that is, they didn't believe in fighting war. So they assumed that they would be free from harassment from the British soldiers and the Indians. But little Frances' eldest brother, eighteen-year-old Giles Slocum, had disobeyed their father's order to leave the British and Indians alone. Giles and some of his friends joined other white settlers in fighting to protect their homes. The Indians felt betrayed.

So when little Frances was having fun outdoors on that November morning in 1778, the peace was suddenly shattered. A gunshot startled everyone. The older neighbor boy—the one wearing the army coat—dropped dead. Frances' mother screamed to the other children that they should hide in the woods. Delaware Indians began to search the Slocums' cabin. They discovered Frances, who was desperately trying to hide. The Indians also found one of her brothers, who was handicapped and couldn't run. The Indians picked up the Slocum children—including the surviving neighbor boy—and started to carry them away.

Frances' mother ran from her hiding place in the woods and shouted that one of her sons was disabled and couldn't walk. The Indians let him go. Then Frances began screaming for her mother. A Delaware brave slung the little girl over his shoulder and disappeared into the woods with her. Other Indians carried the neighbor boy.

For almost sixty years, none of the white settlers knew what had happened to little Frances Slocum. Her mother spent the rest of her life trying to find her, but always failed. About six years after the kidnapping, the neighbor boy who had been taken with Frances returned to the white settlers. He told everyone that the Delaware were treating Frances kindly, but her family remained upset.

Tales and rumors about the lost "little sister" of the Wyoming Valley spread across the American frontier. After fifty-five years, though, even Frances' brothers and sisters assumed she was dead.

Then in the 1830s, a young trader named George Washington Ewing was traveling by horseback across Indiana. One night, Ewing was bargaining with Miami Indians in Deaf Man's Village, a town on the Mississinewa River not far from the modern Indiana city of **Peru**.

Exhausted and cold, Ewing decided not to return to his home in **Logansport** that night. Because he was friendly with many of the Indians, Ewing decided to stay overnight in a two-story log house of a Miami family.

Joining the family circle, Ewing settled near the fireplace and chatted in the Miami language, which he spoke very well. Although he enjoyed talking to the Miami men, Ewing was particularly intrigued by one of the women—a mysterious, feeble widow.

The elderly woman seemed to run the household. Ewing noticed that she had auburn hair, unusual for a Native American.

Slowly, the other family members said good night to their guest and went to bed. The elderly widow sat still, staring at the open fireplace. Ewing was about to go to bed when she asked him to wait.

She explained that she was ill and might die soon. But she wanted to share a secret. The elderly woman then told him an amazing story about having been born to white parents, but carried away as a child by Delaware Indians. She had forgotten her first name, but her father's name was Slocum. The Indians called her Maconaquah. They treated her with love and warmth, as if she had been born to them.

She had married twice. He first husband was a Delaware. Her second husband, a Miami chief, had become deaf (that's why the town was called Deaf Man's Village), and then had died.

The old woman begged Ewing not to reveal her secret. She was terrified that white people—maybe some of her relatives—would force her to leave her home and her Miami family.

At first, Ewing promised to protect

her. But when he returned to Logansport the next day, he decided that her family members should be told. They would want to know about her, he decided. So he tracked them down. Ewing sent details about the "white Indian" woman named Slocum to people in the Pennsylvania towns closest to the frontier area that she had described.

The news about the "lost sister" eventually reached the Slocums. Astonished and anxious to see Frances, two of her brothers and a sister traveled to Indiana in 1837. With an interpreter—someone who could speak the Miami language—the Slocums went to Deaf Man's Village.

They quickly determined that the old woman was Frances. During their childhood, one of the brothers had damaged Frances' finger while they were playing in a blacksmith shop. The old woman happened to mention the long-ago accident—and even displayed her marred finger.

Her brothers and sister assumed she would want to return to Pennsylvania with them. Frances refused. She explained that her husband, on his deathbed, asked her to always live with his people. The Indians had always treated her with kindness, she said. Besides, she enjoyed her home and land in Indiana.

The Slocums asked her to at least come to Pennsylvania for a visit. Again, Frances declined. She explained that she would not know the white people's customs—that is, how to behave among them. She also was frail and worried that she might die during the trip. Frances wanted to pass away among the Miami.

A few days later, the Slocums left. Despite her fears that she was near death, Frances lived several more years. They were years of many more cultural changes in Indiana. By the early 1840s, most of the Miami Indians had been moved west of the Mississippi River.

But an order passed by the U.S. Congress allowed Frances Slocum and her family to remain in their two-story log cabin near Peru. She died there in 1847 at age seventy-four.

John and William Conner

The Conner brothers were vital links between the American Indians and early white settlers in the Indiana Territory. But that isn't the only reason they are considered to be among Indiana's most important historical figures. The brothers grew up in both the white and Native American cultures, and they were among the first white settlers of what eventually became the Hoosier state.

John and William Conner were born to white parents in a village in the Ohio wilderness—John in 1775 and William two years later in 1777. They had two older brothers and a sister; their oldest brother was named James.

Their mother, Margaret, had been captured as a child during an Indian raid. She was raised by the Shawnee. The brothers' father, an adventurous frontiersman named Richard Conner, had to apply to the Shawnee chief to marry Margaret. According to some accounts, he paid two hundred dollars in goods, and the couple had to agree that their first-born son would remain with the tribe. James, who was born in 1771, initially was left with the Shawnee. The Conners were able to get him back when William was a baby.

The family settled in a new town built on the Ohio frontier. The Conners

William Conner, settler and fur trader.

Did you know?

- William Conner had two wives. The first was a Delaware Indian named Mekinges; they had six children. Along with most of the other Delaware Indians in central Indiana, Mekinges and the children moved west of the Mississippi River in 1820. Then, William Conner married Elizabeth Chapman, one of the few single white women in central Indiana. With Elizabeth, he had ten more children. Conner Street in modern, suburban Noblesville is named after William Conner, one of the city's founders.

- Once Indianapolis became the state capital in 1825, John Conner quickly moved there. He opened a successful store, but died just one year later.

joined a religious community primarily of Indians. They freely mingled with various tribes. William and John grew up as "white Indians." Another brother, Henry, was born 1780. Because he was blond, Henry was called "White Hair" by the Indians.

During the Revolutionary War—when the Conner brothers were age ten and younger—the family members felt in danger, along with their neighbors and Indian friends. In 1781, British troops and Indians hostile to the white settlers wanted to shut down all of the Christian churches and religious communities in Ohio. The British feared they were spies for the Americans. Richard and Margaret would get no special treatment just because they had four young boys or because Margaret had lived with the Shawnee.

The Conner family and four hundred neighbors, including Indians and missionaries, were ordered to leave their homes and their crops—even their kettles. They were forced to march north to Detroit—quickly.

On the long march, Richard Conner carried one of his young sons, alternating between John (who was six years old) and William (who was four). Margaret carried the baby, Henry, on her back in what later would become known as "Indian fashion." Legend has it that she even darkened the infant's blond hair so Henry would look more like an Indian and attract less attention to the fact that the Conners were among the few whites in the group.

The Conners marched one hundred and twenty-five miles in twenty days. As their shoes tore to shreds, their feet ached and bled. By the time the Conners and their friends arrived in Detroit, they were exhausted and starving.

Even so, the Conner brothers survived the journey. John and William grew up in what is now the state of Michigan and began trading furs as young men.

In 1800, when the brothers were in their early twenties, they saw wonderful opportunities for fur trading in the wilderness to the south: the Indiana Territory. So they came here to set up trading posts among the Delaware Indians. At the time the Conners arrived, there were almost no white women in central Indiana. Both brothers married Delaware Indians.

John Conner later settled in southeastern Indiana and planned the town of **Connersville**. William founded a post on the White River near what became **Noblesville**, one of three towns that he planned.

William Conner's log cabin became a gathering spot for both Indians and white traders. As a link between the whites and Indians, Conner served as an interpreter for treaties. He helped persuade the Delaware chiefs to give up their lands in central Indiana and move to land west of the Mississippi River.

In 1820, ten political leaders gathered at William Conner's log cabin to plan a new state capital: Indianapolis. The group of leaders—including a general and governor, occasionally—met under trees because Conner's cabin was too cramped to accommodate everyone. For entertainment, they traveled in canoes at night to hunt deer by torchlight.

The group chose Indianapolis as the place for the new capital because of its central location. (**Corydon** in southern Indiana had been serving as the capital since Indiana became a state in 1816).

By the time Indianapolis was up and humming, William Conner's cabin was long gone. He built a two-story brick home along the White River. This house is familiar to thousands of Hoosier children and adults—as well as visitors from around the world. It is on the grounds of **Conner Prairie**, an outdoor living history museum.

William Conner died in 1855, and John Conner in 1826.

Abraham Lincoln

For fourteen important years of his life, **Abraham Lincoln** was a Hoosier. The remarkable man who became the sixteenth president of the United States lived in southern Indiana from age seven to twenty-one. Those are crucial, life-changing years for any person, and young Lincoln was no exception.

"I grew up in Indiana," Abraham Lincoln (1809–1865) said as an adult. In fact, he spent one-fourth of his entire life as a Hoosier.

His family moved here during the same month that Indiana joined the United States of America as the nineteenth state—December 1816. The Lincolns came to southern Indiana from Kentucky, where Abe had been born on February 12, 1809. The family's rugged cabin in Kentucky was only eighteen feet long, with a dirt floor and one window.

In the Indiana wilderness, the Lincolns once again squeezed into a one-room log cabin. And seven-year-old Abe even helped his father, Thomas Lincoln, hack his way through five miles of forest. Although he was skinny and gawky, Abe was unusually tall for his age and could swing an axe. He chopped undergrowth in the Indiana forest while his father felled huge trees for the cabin.

This illustration of Abe Lincoln shows how he probably looked at age nineteen, during his days as a Hoosier. (Illustration by Lloyd Ostendorf)

They built the small home on land they had cleared near towering oak trees that were awe-inspiring and a bit frightening. By the time the Lincolns arrived in the southern Indiana wilderness, Native Americans had left the area. Eventually, about eight other families settled within a mile of the Lincoln cabin. The frontier community came to be known as Little Pigeon Creek.

Young Abe, who had attended school briefly in Kentucky, occasionally attended two or three schools in Indiana. Mostly, though, he learned at home in the cabin. He read the Bible, Shakespeare, and *Robinson Crusoe*. Abe learned simple religious lessons from his kind-hearted mother, Nancy Hanks Lincoln.

A sensitive boy, Abe was inside one day when he saw a flock of wild turkeys approach the Lincoln cabin. His father wasn't home, so Abe asked his mother if he could use Thomas Lincoln's heavy rifle. After she gave permission, Abe stood inside the cabin, struggled with the big weapon, and aimed it through a crack. He pulled the trigger and killed a turkey.

Abe was excited until he ran outdoors and saw the beauty of the bird he had killed. Recalling the experience years later, Abe Lincoln said he was so shaken that he never again "pulled a trigger" on a large animal.

Young Abe and his parents lived in the one-room cabin with a fourth member of the Lincoln family. She was Abe's sister, Sarah, who was about two years older than her brother.

But within three years of the Lincolns' arrival, life in the cabin would be greatly changed. The cabin eventually became home to what we would call today a "blended family"—one that combined three sets of children who had lost one or both parents.

The family tragedies occurred during 1818, when Abe was barely nine years old. Several farmers, including Thomas Lincoln, noticed that their cows were trembling. The farmers began to realize that cows with the "trembles" were suffering from a mysterious sickness. Cows apparently got the disease when they grazed on a poisonous plant called a "white snakeroot."

Horrified, the farmers and their families realized that people were dying after they drank milk from the sick cows. "Milk sickness" began to create panic in frontier communities. It wiped out entire families. Victims became dizzy, intensely thirsty, vomited, and almost always died within a few days.

Nancy Hanks Lincoln was caring for three of the milk sickness victims in the Little Pigeon Creek settlement. One victim was a neighbor, Mrs. Peter Bonna. The other two were relatives of the Lincolns: Nancy's aunt, Elizabeth Sparrow, and Mrs. Sparrow's husband, Thomas. The Sparrows had moved near the Lincolns about a year earlier with a teenager in their care named Dennis Hanks. As the Sparrows died, eighteen-year-old Dennis moved into the Lincoln cabin and shared a loft with young Abe. (Sarah, who was ten, slept below with the adult Lincolns.)

To the family's horror, Nancy began to experience severe symptoms of milk sickness. Feeling helpless, the Lincolns and Dennis could do nothing but watch and try to ease her suffering.

"She knew she was going to die," Dennis Hanks recalled years later. "She called up the children to her dying side and told them to be good and kind to their father, to one another and to the world, expressing a hope that they might live as they had been taught by her to live."

Devastated by her death, the surviving family members buried Nancy Hanks Lincoln in a family plot on a little hill near their cabin. They could see her grave each morning as they stepped out the door. Thomas Lincoln made the coffin for his wife, using wooden pegs that young Abe had whittled.

Bouts of deep sadness fell upon Abraham Lincoln for the rest of his life after the death of his gentle, loving mother. But the challenges of life in the Indiana frontier also made young Abe mentally tough and physically strong. In addition, he learned the importance of a sense of humor in surviving hardships.

His humor also helped him cope

with constant adjustments in his family life. Slightly more than a year after Nancy Hanks Lincoln died, Thomas Lincoln returned to Kentucky looking for a wife—and a mother for Abe and Sarah. He married Sarah Bush Johnston, a widow with three children of her own. The whole brood—including her children, Elizabeth, John, and Matilda—moved into the one-room Lincoln cabin in Indiana.

Just like Abe's mother, his stepmother encouraged his reading. She considered him a wonderful, well-behaved child.

By the time he was fourteen, Abe was making speeches to his sister, stepbrother, stepsisters, and other children who visited. Soon he was telling stories at the fence as other Hoosier farm boys gathered around. In his talks, Lincoln often used jokes to emphasize his points or to cope with the grim realities of frontier life. In time, young Abe was telling stories at the general store and blacksmith shop in Little Pigeon Creek.

Abraham Lincoln would use these storytelling abilities in his later career as a lawyer—and, eventually, as president of the United States.

According to some accounts, while Lincoln was still living in southern Indiana, he began to attend court sessions in Spencer and Perry counties. He would watch the attorneys and analyze their speaking skills.

Abe Lincoln, who grew up to be a towering six feet, four inches tall, also helped his father build a new cabin in the spring of 1829, when young Abe was twenty-one years old.

Their work on the new cabin was interrupted when word came from relatives in Illinois. They informed the Lincolns that milk sickness was rare in that state, and that the land was fine for farming. So the Lincoln family decided to move.

Some Americans tend to focus only on Abraham Lincoln's connections to the states of Illinois and Kentucky, overlooking the important role of Indiana in shaping his character. But there are special places in Indiana where visitors are able to learn a great deal about this important American leader.

In southern Indiana, there is the Lincoln Boyhood National Memorial. It includes the Nancy Hanks Memorial Cemetery, a historical farm and a visitors center. At the other end of the state—in downtown Fort Wayne—there is a popular Lincoln Museum. The museum has exhibits, a library, galleries and displays of some of Abraham Lincoln's possessions, including one of his top hats.

Whom do you consider our greatest president?

Some Americans consider Abraham Lincoln, president from 1861 until his tragic death in 1865, our country's greatest leader ever. He led the country during the most bloody period in our history, the Civil War. Abraham Lincoln became known as the "Great Emancipator" for signing a law that freed the slaves. His term as president was cut short when he was assassinated while attending a play in Washington, D.C. (His funeral train stopped in Indianapolis on its way to the president's burial place in Springfield, Illinois.)

Other Americans consider our greatest president to have been the first person to hold the highest office in the land, George Washington (1732–1799) of Virginia.

Is there another of our presidents you would consider to be the greatest?

Juliet V. Strauss

It's a shame that boys and girls who are different sometimes find themselves mocked and shunned. Why is this?

People often seem like herd animals who reject those who may be different or weak. In a school setting, those "different" people may have good grades—or bad grades. They may have odd mannerisms. As a result, they are called nerds. Other people sometimes make their lives miserable.

That's what happened to **Juliet V. Strauss**, who was shunned because her family was poor and she wore tattered clothes. Her father died when she was just four years old, leaving only her hard-working mother, who was only twenty-eight years old, to raise Juliet and her three sisters in **Rockville**, Indiana. Her mother struggled every day to put food on the table. Instead of feeling sorry for Juliet or offering to help, her neighbors ridiculed her.

Just like the old saying—"Don't get mad, get even!"—Juliet Strauss turned the tables when she grew up and wrote a newspaper column. In the column, she couldn't resist poking fun at the wealthy people of Rockville—the same people who had snubbed her when she was a little girl.

For example, Strauss—who was one of the first woman journalists in Indiana—secretly watched a roller-skating party attended by Rockville's high society. In *The Rockville Tribune* newspaper, she wrote about the "collisions" and "bumped heads" among the awkward young businessmen and their girlfriends as they tried to skate.

That was at the very beginning of the remarkable career of Juliet Strauss (1863–1918), who eventually became one of the best-read magazine writers in the nation. From her home in Rockville, which is in Parke County in far-western Indiana, she wrote a monthly column for *The Ladies' Home Journal*, a hugely popular magazine. Her column, called "The Ideas of a Plain Country Woman," dealt with the hard work—and the joys—of being a homemaker, wife and mother of two daughters.

She also fought to save beautiful Turkey Run State Park and its magnificent trees. As a girl, Strauss often had played in Turkey Run's woods. When she became a well-known writer, she crusaded to protect the trees from being chopped down.

For twenty-five years, Strauss wrote a weekly column for the *The Rockville Tribune*. She even wrote the column when she was sick and in bed.

Strauss signed her column in *The Ladies' Home Journal* "The Country Contributor." The column began appearing in 1905, when the *Journal* was the leading women's magazine in the country. In one column, she described the routine of a typically exhausting day for her. It included cooking, cleaning, ironing, baking, feeding the chickens, canning, comforting a sobbing child, helping a friend with three crying babies, and putting her own children to bed.

Strauss' writing was admired by the most popular Indiana literary figure of the time, poet James Whitcomb Riley. The two became good friends; Riley praised Strauss's book, *The Ideas of a Plain Country Woman* (1908).

After Strauss died, women journalists across Indiana arranged for a statue in her honor to be placed in Turkey Run State Park, which she loved so much. That statue was the state's first memorial ever erected to honor a woman.

Other famous women writers from Indiana

Jessamyn West

Would you drink a potion of orange juice and raw eggs?

Another famous writer who grew up in Indiana, Jessamyn West, drank that gross mixture when she was seriously ill. West (1902–1984) was from Jennings County in southern Indiana. She was stricken with tuberculosis when she was studying for her final exams for a Ph.D. (doctoral degree).

Her mother thought a mixture of orange juice and raw eggs would build up Jessamyn's strength. Although she had been given up for dead in 1931, her mother nursed her back to health by feeding her constantly and making her drink the juice-and-egg mixture.

Jessamyn enjoyed a full recovery and went on to write many popular novels and collections of short stories, including several set in southern Indiana. Her most famous book, *Friendly Persuasion* (1945), was about peace-loving Quakers in Indiana who struggled with whether to fight in the Civil War.

Emily Kimbrough

Juliet Strauss wasn't the only Hoosier to influence the pages of *The Ladies' Home Journal*. In the 1920s, one of the magazine's top editors was Emily Kimbrough, a well-known writer from Muncie.

Kimbrough (1899–1989) was famous for a best-selling book that she co-wrote with her best friend from college, actress Cornelia Otis Skinner. Their book, *Our Hearts Were Young and Gay* (1942), described their adventures on an ocean liner and a vacation trip to Europe in the early 1920s. In one funny episode in the book, the young women climb the bell tower of an old cathedral in France. Frightened of heights, they scare each other in a dream episode by imagining that they are locked in the tower. The only way the women can summon help is to take off many of their clothes and fling them from a balcony so people on the street below realize they're trapped inside. In the nightmare, the women are in their underwear when rescuers finally arrive.

Our Hearts Were Young and Gay was made into a Hollywood movie, and Kimbrough went on to write thirteen more books. At *The Ladies' Home Journal*, she was managing editor and fashion editor.

A happy—and healthy—Jessamyn West. (Photofest)

From *Our Hearts Were Young and Gay*

In one chapter of *Our Hearts Were Young and Gay* (1942), the two authors wrote about a miserable night they spent as college students traveling in Europe. Staying at what they assumed was a pleasant, clean hotel in France, the girls managed to fall asleep, even though they were excited because two handsome young men planned to visit them in the morning.

But here's what happened in the middle of the night, according to a section in the book that was written from Cornelia's point of view:

"BEDBUGS!" I shrieked and fell back on the pillow . . . "I always get bitten and it's always on the face! Every species of the insect kingdom bites me. Fleas, spiders, flies . . . even moths! And they never bite me anywhere but on the face!"

"Maybe it's the perfume you use," Emily suggested . . . "We've got to go to the American drug store," she said, and leapt out of bed. "They will tell us what to do . . ."

I was a horrifying sight to behold. My great, blown-out lip gleamed brighter than ever before . . . Whenever I caught a glimpse of myself in a mirror, I moaned and looked hastily away . . . We leapt into a taxi, telling the driver to go as fast as possible.

The girls smeared a lotion on Cornelia's face. Then they scrubbed their hotel room with Lysol so their boyfriends wouldn't notice the bedbugs and other insects. Emily and Cornelia managed to enjoy their dates without embarrassing themselves—but many other funny adventures and close calls in the book don't end so happily.

James Dean

Some people called James Dean a rebel, a daredevil, and a loner. To others, the talented movie star who grew up in **Fairmount**, Indiana, was loaded with charisma—a young man who simply yearned to be loved. One thing everyone agrees on: Almost no one else in the history of movies and television has had a more lasting impact on audiences.

Around the world, James Dean has become a symbol of "cool"—and of the pain, sensitivity and confusion that can be part of life for teenagers. The image of this legendary Hoosier—usually in a red windbreaker jacket, white T-shirt and, blue jeans—adorns everything from posters, coffee mugs and license plates to U.S. postage stamps. The only other entertainers whose images come close in popularity are those of two other stars from the 1950s, singer Elvis Presley and actress Marilyn Monroe.

Amazingly enough, James Dean inspired all of this adoration by starring in only three movies. He also had small roles in two other films, and had fascinated audiences with his powerful performances in several TV dramas before he died in a car crash in 1955. James Dean was just twenty-four years old when he was killed.

He was born in Marion, Indiana, in

James Dean in a standard studio pose. (Photofest)

Dean's performance in *East of Eden* (1954) made him famous. (Photofest)

1931. When the boy known as "Jimmy" was just five years old, he moved to California with his parents, Winton and Mildred Dean. By all accounts, young Jimmy was devoted to his mother. At age nine, he was shattered when she died of cancer. Unable to care for his son by himself, Winton Dean sent Jimmy back to Indiana to live with his aunt and uncle, Ortense and Marcus Winslow. Jimmy grew up with them on a farm near Fairmount, a small town ten miles from Marion.

At Fairmount High School, Dean made a name for himself in a couple of ways. Even though he was not tall (at his full adult height, he stood barely five feet, eight inches in boots), Jim excelled as a basketball player. Even more, he excelled in speech competitions. Displaying the outstanding dramatic ability that later would thrill movie audiences, Dean won the state speech championship in 1949, his senior year of high school.

"Part of his secret, part of his success, was that anything he wanted to do, he did well," his drama coach, Adeline Nall, recalled years later. "He surely had the ability to concentrate."

After graduating from Fairmount High, Dean moved to California. He briefly attended two colleges, made a Pepsi commercial and had small parts in two movies: *Sailor Beware* (1951) and *Has Anybody Seen My Gal?* (1952).

But James Dean didn't come to public attention until after he made his next move: He came to New York City,

studied acting and created a sensation with his performances in two Broadway plays. He also captured people's attention in several TV dramas, including one about the life of another famous American with Hoosier roots: Abraham Lincoln. (In a 1952 TV special, Dean played a Union soldier who is spared from being court-martialed by President Lincoln. Dean's character breaks down as he tells the president about his concern for his widowed mother.)

Movie directors couldn't ignore James Dean's talent. His acting style came across as remarkably "natural" and fresh. Dean was brought to Hollywood to make the three movies that made him legendary. The films are:

East of Eden (1954), in which Dean played a misunderstood young man searching for his mother. He was nominated for an Academy Award for this movie, which was based on a classic novel by John Steinbeck.

Rebel Without a Cause (1955), which starred Dean as a teenager who becomes an outcast when he enters a new high school.

Giant (1956), in which he played a free-spirited cowboy who strikes oil.

The boots that Dean wore in *Giant* are exhibited, along with his motorcycle, at the Fairmount Historical Museum. It's one of two museums in Fairmount devoted to the town's most famous "son." The other museum, the

The image of James Dean, which is controlled by the Indianapolis-based business of CMG Worldwide, is featured on everything from U.S. postage stamps (shown here) to posters, coffee mugs and license plates.

James Dean Gallery, displays his high school yearbooks, movie costumes, and posters from around the world.

Every year on September 30, the anniversary of Dean's tragic death, thousands of people from across the country visit Fairmount for the "Remembering James Dean Festival." It includes a parade and an auto show featuring hundreds of 1950s convertibles and other classic cars.

James Dean was driving a silver Porsche sports car when he was killed; he was on his way to compete in a race. He's buried in the Winslow family plot in Park Cemetery near Fairmount. James Dean's grave and hometown have been visited by thousands of fans—including fellow actors who considered the young Hoosier a genius.

Richard Lugar

Ever since his days at Shortridge High School in Indianapolis, Richard Lugar has been a leader of his peers. One of his Shortridge classmates, future author Dan Wakefield, said upon meeting Dick Lugar: "I assumed he was going to be president of the United States someday."

That hasn't happened, although Richard Lugar ran for the Republican nomination for president in 1996. However, almost every other top honor has come Dick Lugar's way—from Eagle Scout to Rhodes Scholar (it's awarded to the country's best and brightest college students) to American statesman.

As a U.S. senator from Indiana since 1976, he has been one of the top experts in foreign policy. The Hoosier politician seems forever "on call" to advise presidents—and the American people—when a crisis erupts in far-away places such as the Balkans in Europe or the Philippines in Asia.

In an interview in his office on Capitol Hill, Dick Lugar (who was born in 1932) was able to recall every detail of his introduction to politics. It was on Monument Circle in downtown Indianapolis. He was an eight-year-old boy in the middle of a huge, cheering crowd.

From the balcony of a hotel on that day in 1940, Hoosier presidential candidate Wendell Willkie delivered a rousing speech. Dick Lugar recalled not only being excited by politics, but by his hometown: "Through my youthful eyes, Indianapolis . . . appeared wondrous," he said.

Dick Lugar would grow up to lead his hometown as mayor from 1967 until 1975. First, though, he made a name for himself as a student and role model.

As a boy, he was a Sunday school regular at Central Avenue United Methodist Church. (An active Methodist as an adult, Senator Lugar is a frequent lay minister at churches across Indiana.) At Shortridge, Lugar and novelist-to-be Dan Wakefield were co-sports editors of *The Echo*, the school's famous daily newspaper. Lugar also was valedictorian—that is, the top academic student—of the Class of 1950.

Richard Lugar, U.S. senator and former mayor of Indianapolis. (Courtesy of the office of U.S. Senator Richard Lugar)

Then he attended Denison University in Ohio, where he shared the class presidency with Charlene Schmeltzer. The two married in 1956.

In the late 1950s, Dick Lugar was an intelligence officer in the U.S. Navy.

He regularly got up at 2:30 A.M. to memorize overnight reports from around the world.

He brought that same work ethic back to Marion County, Indiana, where he inherited a corn, soybean, and wheat farm of six hundred acres. Dick Lugar also helped run a family business that makes baking equipment and food machinery.

His political career started in 1964 as a member of the Indianapolis Public Schools board.

"Wouldn't it be a great thing if Dick Lugar were mayor?" a newspaper columnist asked.

Soon he was. As mayor, Lugar initiated a change considered "radical": In 1970, he blended many offices of the city of Indianapolis and Marion County. It gave the city and county a joint form of government known as "Unigov." In one swoop, Indianapolis went from being the nation's twenty-sixth largest city to the twelfth largest.

Magazines such as *Newsweek* called Dick Lugar "the Hoosier hotshot." They praised him for improving the image of Indianapolis, which once had been ridiculed as "Naptown" and "India-NO-Place."

The young mayor also drew attention as a physical fitness advocate—he's an avid jogger—years and years before it became trendy.

In a different type of running—political campaigning—his 1996 race for the presidential nomination was a rare loss. In 1994, Richard Lugar made Indiana history by winning a fourth straight term to the U.S. Senate. No other Hoosier has done that.

In 2000, he topped himself: Richard Lugar was elected to a fifth term. Also that year Senator Lugar was nominated for one of the world's most prestigious honors, the Nobel Peace Prize. He didn't win the prize, but the nomination was powerful recognition for his work (teamed with a Democratic senator from Georgia) to reduce nuclear weapons in the former Soviet Union.

Wendell Willkie

The candidate for president who inspired young Dick Lugar from the hotel balcony in 1940 was an unusual politician in many ways.

Wendell Willkie of Elwood, Indiana, had been a Democrat for most of his life, and then switched to the Republican Party a few years before the presidential race. Willkie (1892–1944) was a "dark horse" candidate—that is, an unexpected and unlikely one. A successful businessman, he had never been elected to any office—not governor, mayor or even county clerk—before Republicans chose him to take on popular President Franklin D. Roosevelt.

"We want Willkie! We want Willkie! We want Willkie!" people chanted at the 1940 Republican convention.

Their man had led an adventurous life. As Willkie was growing up in Elwood, his family fell on hard times. To earn money, he worked for a junk dealer (his job was to remove nails from trash), drove a bakery wagon and was a cook at a diner. Eventually, he became a successful lawyer—and a wealthy one.

Wendell Willkie, 1940 presidential candidate. (Bachrach, courtesy of Indiana State Archives)

Willkie ran his whirlwind presidential campaign out of a hotel in Rushville, his wife's hometown. After he was defeated by his arch-rival President Roosevelt, the two became friends.

A blunt man, Willkie always took pride in saying what he believed—whether it bothered Republicans or Democrats, friends or enemies.

"I'd rather be right than president," he said several times.

Oscar Robertson

Long before he turned twenty-one years old, **Oscar Robertson** was a trailblazer in **Indianapolis**.

The basketball star known to thousands of fans as "the Big O" led the first team of black players to win the state championship in1955. The next year, Oscar Robertson's team from the legendary Crispus Attucks High School did it again. Not only was Oscar's team the first African-American squad to capture the tournament title, his was the first team from any Indianapolis high school to do so. Young Oscar, who was born in 1938, led these dynamic, championship teams during an era of widespread racial segregation.

"I used to look up at airplanes and wonder where in the world they were going," he wrote later in life, recalling his days as a seven-year-old in a low-income neighborhood. Oscar was born in Charlotte, Tennessee, but his family moved to Indianapolis when he was a child. He grew up just west of downtown in Lockefield Gardens, which then (the late 1940s and early fifties) was a poverty-stricken housing project. Later, Robertson would refer to the neighborhood as a "ghetto."

Yet Robertson found some positive

Oscar Robertson (center) posed with two other "Mr. Basketballs"—Bob Masters and Bobby Plump—at young Oscar's ceremony in 1956. (From the collection of the Indiana State Museum and Historical Sites)

aspects about life in his adopted hometown.

"I was fortunate to grow up in Indianapolis, an environment where people took basketball seriously," Robertson wrote in *Oscar Robertson: The Art of Basketball*. "At an early age, I saw that if I wanted to play with older, more experienced players, I'd have to practice on my own to bring my skills up to their level. They weren't running a clinic, and they weren't about to let anybody on the court who would slow them down.

"That was my first lesson: The best way to improve is to play with people who are better than you."

Always proud, outspoken and hard working, Robertson improved rapidly and began playing basketball for Attucks High School in 1952. (Only four years earlier, an Indiana University basketball star from Shelbyville named **Bill Garrett** had become the first black player in the Big Ten group of colleges.)

Attucks High School had basketball heroes before Oscar Robertson. They included his older brother, Bailey Robertson, as well as such outstanding players as Hallie Bryant, Willie Merriwether, and Willie Gardner.

But none became as big a star as "the Big O." Robertson, who is six feet, five inches tall, played guard and led Attucks to an amazing run of forty-eight straight victories; in addition to Oscar, the team's coach, **Ray Crowe**, became a star. The Attucks team captured its first state championship by beating another all-black high school, Gary Roosevelt High School, in 1955.

After graduating from Attucks, Robertson became college basketball's all-time leading scorer at the University of Cincinnati. His scoring total of 2,973 points set a national record that remained in place for ten years. Robertson was named to the All-America team in 1958, 1959, and 1960.

Also in 1960, Oscar traveled to Rome as co-captain of the U.S. Olympic team. His team ended up winning the gold medal.

As a professional player in the National Basketball Association, Oscar Robertson played ten seasons with the Cincinnati Royals (Robertson was named Rookie of the Year his first season) and four seasons with the Milwaukee Bucks. He helped propel the Bucks to the NBA championship in 1974.

For most of his adult life, Robertson has lived in Cincinnati. He made headlines in 1997 for a dramatic act of kindness. "The Big O" donated one of his kidneys to his daughter, Tia. She suffers from lupus, a disease that affects the body's organs. Robertson and his wife, Yvonne, have two other daughters, Shana and Mari.

Jeff Gordon

Residents of Pittsboro, a small town in Hendricks County, Indiana, are adjusting to gawkers, TV crews, fan club members and curious tourists from as far away as Texas and Tennessee.

That's because the small town of just 1,080 people was the boyhood hometown of a genuine superstar in stock car racing. As a resident of Pittsboro, which is about fifteen miles west of Indianapolis, teenage Jeff Gordon saw his career in racing really take off with a roar. It's doubtful, though, that even young Gordon imagined he quickly would become such a major celebrity that NASCAR officials call him a "living legend," a hugely popular athlete who often comes close to dominating his sport.

An early wake-up call to the talents of the clean-cut, handsome driver with Hoosier roots came in August 1994 with his thrilling victory in the very first Brickyard 400 at the Indianapolis Motor Speedway. Jeff Gordon's win there was almost too perfect: The first stock car race at the Speedway was won by this personable driver who graduated from a nearby high school and who was engaged to marry a beauty queen he'd met on Valentine's Day. To top it off, Gordon won the Brickyard 400 only a few days after he turned twenty-three.

Jeff Gordon in his moment of triumph in 1994 after winning the first Brickyard 400 at the Indianapolis Motor Speedway. (Indianapolis Motor Speedway)

That victory, of course, turned out to be only a beginning. In successes that came so rapidly that racing experts called the pattern "phenomenal," Gordon zoomed past every competitor to win NASCAR's prestigious Winston Cup (stock car's top series) three times—in 1995, 1997, and 1998. In 1995, when Gordon first captured the Winston Cup (given to the NASCAR driver who has won the most points in races during an entire season), he became the youngest champion in what's known as NASCAR's "modern era." Gordon, just twenty-four, was attracting thousands of new spectators to stock car racing with his charisma and his rainbow-colored Dupont Chevy cars.

In Pittsboro, where Gordon lived

from age fourteen through his early twenties, his image (as well as the rainbow colors and "24," his car number) adorns everything from Christmas ornaments and lamps to license plates and balloons. Even residents of Lizton, a town just west of Pittsboro, feel a sense of "ownership" of Jeff Gordon. That's because Tri-West High School, where Gordon was prom king and a member of the Class of 1989, is in Lizton. And the trilevel house that was Gordon's boyhood home actually is between Lizton and Pittsboro.

The future star was born August 4, 1971 in Vallejo, California. Gordon started racing as a five-year-old, beginning with miniature race cars called "quarter midgets," small, open-wheeled cars with a motor of less than three horsepower. By the late 1970s, he was a national champion among quarter-midget drivers; he followed that up by winning dozens of Go-Kart races.

Then Gordon's mother and stepfather, Carol and John Bickford, decided that, primarily to advance their son's racing career, the family should move from California to central Indiana. By then—the mid-1980s—fourteen-year-old Jeff was competing in sprint cars; many of the dirt and paved tracks are in the Midwest. So the family settled in Pittsboro, where Jeff's stepfather set up an auto parts business in the family home.

With his family, young Gordon tried to live a normal life away from

Another new star in auto racing: Tony Stewart

"When you grow up forty-five minutes from the Indianapolis Motor Speedway, and all your life every May when you got home from school and the first thing you did was turn on the TV to watch practice at Indy . . ."

That's how talented young race driver Tony Stewart of Columbus, Indiana, began a diary account for *USA Today* of his month of May in 2001. Stewart, one of the brightest stars in auto racing since the mid-1990s, was attempting in the diary to explain the importance to him of winning the Indianapolis 500; he has called a victory there "the Number One goal in my life."

So far, Stewart, who was born in 1971, hasn't won the 500-Mile Race. But he's won dozens of other races, trophies and awards and competed with distinction in several different racing circuits—from small cars (sprint cars and midgets) to NASCAR (stock cars) to open-wheel Indy cars. By the late 1990s Anthony Wayne Stewart (that's his full name) was being called "America's most diverse race car driver."

His victories began in Go-Kart racing while he was growing up in Columbus and Rushville, Indiana. By the time Stewart graduated from Columbus North High School in 1989, he was a world kart champion. Then he became one of the most impressive new drivers in Indy car racing. Tony Stewart captured the pole position in his rookie Indianapolis 500 in 1996; that year, he was named Rookie of the Year at the Speedway. In 1997, he led the 500 for sixty-four laps—more than any other driver—before brushing the fourth-turn wall and finishing fifth. Also that year, Stewart won the Indy Racing League championship and became something of a poster boy for the league.

Through it all, Stewart has developed a reputation for being a bit hot-headed (he has clashed with other drivers), but also as a driver who is intensely proud of his Hoosier roots. Since reaping national fame, Stewart has chosen to live in Columbus—and even purchased his boyhood home.

Not that he's there much. Following the lead of fellow Hoosier race driver John Andretti, Tony Stewart has twice (in 2001 and 1999) pulled off a grueling feat: He competed in two major races six hundred miles apart on the same day, driving in the Indy 500 in the morning and, after flying to North Carolina, racing in a NASCAR race (the Coca-Cola 600) in the late afternoon.

As a stock car driver, Tony Stewart blossomed quickly; he has won ten races in NASCAR's Winston Cup series. In 1999, Tony Stewart was named Winston Cup Rookie of the Year. His fan club grew from 450 members to more than 5,500.

Fun fact: Find Tony Stewart's World Wide Web page at www.tonystewart.com.

racing and frequently ate lunch at Frank and Mary's Restaurant on Main Street in Pittsboro. (**Fun fact:** Gordon almost always ordered a smoked sausage sandwich and apple pie à la mode.) Mostly, though, he focused on racing, and his determination paid off. During his senior year at Tri-West, Gordon was named the U.S. Auto Club's "Rookie of the Year" in midget racing.

By the early 1990s, Gordon was competing on NASCAR's Busch Grand National Series, a stock car circuit one step below the top Winston Cup. Because NASCAR is based in North Carolina, Gordon and the Bickfords separately moved there from Indiana in the early '90s. In 1992 Gordon made his Winston Cup debut at age twenty-one.

At a qualifying race for the Daytona 500 in 1993, Gordon met his future wife, Brooke Sealy, who was serving as Miss Winston. The two dated secretly because sponsors frowned on race queens becoming romantically involved with drivers. Jeff and Brooke married a few months after his historic victory at the first Brickyard 400—a win that *The Indianapolis Star* called "a made-for-TV script that would have

left Walt Disney with a lump in his throat."

In TV interviews, public appearances and speeches after his victories ever since then (his triumphs have included winning the Daytona 500 in 1997), Gordon often talks about his spiritual side. He emphasizes his faith in God as well as the importance of teamwork, sharing credit with his crewmembers. (They have become known as the "Rainbow Warriors.")

His popularity as a role model has resulted in extensive celebrity endorsements; Gordon, who doesn't smoke or drink alcohol, has been featured in TV commercials for Pepsi and been named one of the "Fifty Most Beautiful People in the World" by *People* magazine.

In August of 1999—just before the sixth annual Brickyard 400—Jeff Gordon returned to his boyhood hometown for a special ceremony. Residents of Pittsboro named a stretch of a county road in his honor.

(**Another fun fact:** When Gordon was competing in sprint car races as a fourteen-year-old, he was too young to get an Indiana driver's license. So his mom drove him from their Pittsboro home to his races.)

Tony Stewart, Indy car and stock car driver. (Stephen Baker)

Joshua Bell

By the time he was fourteen years old, talented Joshua Bell of Bloomington already was being praised by music critics across the country. Also by age fourteen, Joshua had won his first major international violin competition and had played at Carnegie Hall, the dream of most classical musicians.

This handsome, dark-haired boy from Indiana obviously was on a fast track to worldwide stardom. Though long described as a "child prodigy," Joshua says he always disliked that phrase because it implied he focused only on music. Proud of being well rounded, Joshua loves video games, pinball, tennis (he was an Indiana tennis champion at age ten) and cheering for Indiana University's basketball team.

"Josh never spent hours and hours in the practice room because he had so many other interests," says Shirley Bell, his mom. She points out that some of those interests, like tennis and other sports, could have injured his wrists or hands—and affected his violin playing. "My husband and I never blocked him from doing anything he wanted to do, including skiing . . . as much as I would have liked him to stop. We just thought having other interests was healthy."

But Shirley Bell and her husband,

Joshua Bell, star violinist. (IMG Artists)

Alan, an IU psychologist, did notice early on that Josh was blessed with rare musical gifts. Joshua, who was born in 1967, took up the violin at age five. Fortunately, there was a brilliant violin teacher in the neighborhood. Josef Gingold (1909–1995), a famous IU professor, took on Joshua as a student when the boy was twelve—which was highly unusual for one of the world's most respected music teachers.

"Joshua was born with great talent," Professor Gingold recalled in an interview. "He later developed tremendous desire to work toward perfection . . . Joshua always has been a joy to teach."

Today, Joshua Bell performs in concerts with leading orchestras around the world—from the London Philharmonic and the Boston Pops to orchestras in Japan, Hong Kong, Switzerland, and Spain. He lives in New York City, but is usually traveling because he's in such demand. Bell performs about 120 concerts every year, regularly starring at many of the top music festivals and almost always winning rave reviews.

For much of the 1990s and so far this century, Bell has been classical music's version of a teen idol. At one point, his record company featured Josh on posters wearing jeans and sneakers and leaning on his car, a flashy Porsche—with his violin under his arm. For several years, Bell performed with a rare, guitar-shaped

Stradivarius violin made in 1726. In recent years, he has upgraded to an even more spectacular Stradivarius; Stradivarius violins are considered the world's best (and most expensive) violins. His is valued at $2.5 million.

With his appeal to young people, Bell became one of the first classical musicians to be the focus of a music video. To top it all off, he has twice been named by *People* magazine as one of the "Fifty Most Beautiful People in the World."

He even has made an impact on film. In 1999, he performed on the Oscar-winning soundtrack of the movie *The Red Violin*. Bell had a small role in the movie as, of course, a violinist. At the Academy Awards ceremony, the film's composer praised him for playing the violin "like a god."

Bell has appeared on such TV programs as *The Tonight Show* and the Arts & Entertainment Network's *Biography* series. As a result, experts and older musicians credit him with introducing classical music to thousands of people—including teenagers and children—who otherwise might not have paid attention to it or learned to love it as Joshua Bell so obviously does.

Ryan White

Ryan White was a teenage crusader who grew up near **Kokomo** and became famous around the world. In 1985, when he was just fourteen and in seventh grade, Ryan became a symbol of courage, dedication, and tolerance because he fought to attend school—and be treated as a regular kid—even though he had a deadly disorder called AIDS.

Parents, children and other people who were terrified of AIDS tried to block Ryan from attending Western Middle School in Howard County—although Indiana health officials were assuring them that there was no reason to be frightened of Ryan. When he was born in 1971, Ryan was diagnosed with hemophilia, a disorder in which the blood does not clot. He was afflicted with AIDS during a blood transfusion in the early 1980s.

Although he was short, frail, and frequently exhausted, Ryan tried to live a normal life. He loved *X-Men* comic books, the Chicago Cubs baseball team and swimming. He had a pet dog and cat.

"I'm getting ready to go to a skating party right now," he said, smiling broadly during an interview at his home in Kokomo.

Ryan White and his mother, Jeanne, at their Kokomo home in 1986, during his crusade to attend school. (Courtesy of *The Indianapolis Star*)

In many ways, though, Ryan's short life was far from typical. He testified before panels of politicians, crusaded with celebrities and appeared on national TV talk shows in his campaign to show that there was no reason to fear, hate or isolate people with AIDS.

In 1987, Ryan moved with his mother, Jeanne White, and his older sister, Andrea, from the Kokomo area to Cicero in Hamilton County. At Hamilton Heights High School in nearby Arcadia, Ryan enjoyed many friends.

His illness gradually became worse, though. In 1990, Ryan died in Riley Hospital for Children in Indianapolis. He was just eighteen years old. Ryan's funeral was attended by rock stars, politicians, TV celebrities, and hundreds of average people who admired his bravery.

Some facts about AIDS

AIDS stands for "acquired immune deficiency syndrome."

It's a disease that damages the body's immune system, which is the system that helps fight illness. When people's immune systems are damaged, they are more likely to become sick from illnesses that wouldn't hurt healthy people.

AIDS is a disease that's harder to get than the cold or the flu. In fact, it's very important to know how people *don't* get AIDS. You can't get it from hugging, kissing or holding hands. It's not spread by coughing or sneezing. The virus that causes AIDS is spread by people's body fluids, including blood.

Ryan White was infected with AIDS from a blood transfusion in a hospital. The blood transfusion occurred in the early 1980s, before people were aware of the risk of spreading AIDS—or even knew much about it at all. In the years since Ryan became infected, health care workers have taken great care to protect the blood supply used by hospitals.

Right now, there is no cure for AIDS. Millions of people have died from it around the world. But doctors and scientists are working on finding a cure, and there are several medications that can help people infected with the virus that causes AIDS.

If you have questions about AIDS, talk to an adult—your parents, a doctor, a health teacher or another teacher, a minister, priest, or rabbi.

(Information courtesy of KidsHealth, a service of the Nemours Foundation, a nonprofit organization devoted to children's health. The foundation focuses on pediatric work and operates several children's hospitals and clinics in the United States.)

Some facts about Ryan White

- Ryan White's struggle to attend school in Indiana was turned into a TV movie in 1987 called *The Ryan White Story*. Although an actor portrays him in the movie, Ryan appears in a small role as another boy who has AIDS.

- His celebrity friends included rock stars Elton John and Michael Jackson as well as Olympic gold medalist Greg Louganis, the best diver in history. When Louganis won a gold medal at the Pan American Games in Indianapolis in 1987, he gave the medal to Ryan.

- Since Ryan's death, his mother, Jeanne White, has carried on his crusade for AIDS education around the world. She had divorced Ryan's dad when their son was a young boy. Two years after Ryan died, Jeanne married a former auto mechanic in Cicero named Roy Ginder. He had befriended Ryan by helping him tune up his prized possession, a red Mustang given to him by Michael Jackson.

Legends in Sports

Baseball legends

The state of Indiana doesn't have a major-league baseball team. The Indianapolis Indians, who play at Victory Field in downtown Indianapolis, are in pro baseball's minor leagues.

Even so, Indiana can claim several major-league baseball stars who have grown up here during the past one hundred years.

The first was **Mordecai "Three-Finger" Brown** (1876–1948), who was considered the greatest pitcher in Chicago Cubs history. Brown grew up in **Nyesville**, a small town in western Indiana. His nickname derived from a childhood accident with a corn shredder in which he lost part of his right hand. Brown went on to be the star of a Cubs dynasty in baseball from 1906 to 1910 that included a World Series championship in 1908.

About twenty-five years later, another Hoosier became a famous player for the Chicago Cubs and other teams. **Billy Herman** (1909–1992), who was born in **New Albany**, played in the 1930s and was one of the greatest hit-and-run hitters of all time.

Two Hoosiers also became stars playing for the Brooklyn (New York) Dodgers, a team that later moved to the West Coast and became the Los Angeles Dodgers. The first was **Gil Hodges** (1924–1972), who grew up in

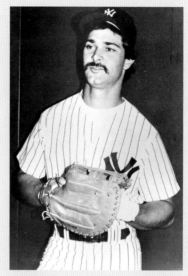
Family lore has it that Don Mattingly had a perfect swing at age eight. (Photofest)

Mordecai "Three-Finger" Brown became a star despite an injury from a farming accident as a boy. (Desperate Enterprises, courtesy of W. C. Madden)

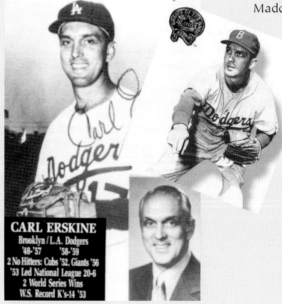

CARL ERSKINE
Brooklyn / L.A. Dodgers
'48-'57   '58-'59
2 No Hitters: Cubs '32, Giants '56
'53 Led National League 20-6
2 World Series Wins
W.S. Record K's-14 '53

Anderson, Indiana, native Carl Erskine was a star pitcher for the Brooklyn Dodgers (now the Los Angeles Dodgers) in the 1950s. After retiring from baseball, Erskine moved back to his hometown. He shares these baseball cards with children when he speaks at schools. (Courtesy of Carl Erskine)

Princeton as the son of a coal miner. Long after playing for the Dodgers, Hodges became a manager for the New York Mets. They were the laughingstock of baseball until Hodges guided the "Miracle Mets" to a World Series championship in 1969.

The second famous Hoosier to play for the Dodgers was **Carl Erskine**. Beginning as a high school baseball star in his hometown of **Anderson**, Erskine (1926–) became a star pitcher for the Dodgers in the 1950s. He then returned to Anderson for a second career as a banker and community leader.

More recently, Evansville native **Don Mattingly** (1961–) was a fan favorite for the New York Yankees as a first baseman. The Yankees drafted Mattingly after he graduated from Reitz Memorial High School, where he was a star pitcher and led the team to a state championship. His heyday with the Yankees was in the 1980s and early '90s.

Victory Field in downtown Indianapolis is known as one of the best minor-league ballparks in the country. (Stephen Baker)

Did you know?

- Ironically, Mordecai "Three-Finger" Brown may have been helped by his reshaped right hand. Because of his unusual hand, he was able to throw a curveball with a sharp downward break.

- During his eighteen seasons in the major leagues, Gil Hodges hit fourteen grand slams, a record. (A batter accomplishes a grand slam when the bases are loaded and he hits a home run—meaning everyone on a base scores, along with the hitter.)

- When the legendary Brooklyn Dodgers moved to Los Angeles in 1958, it was Hoosier Carl Erskine who had the honor of throwing out the first pitch at the new stadium in California.

Kenesaw Mountain Landis

Probably the most famous Hoosier in baseball history wasn't a player. He was the sport's first commissioner.

He had a strange name: Kenesaw Mountain Landis. Landis (1866–1944) was named after a famous battle of the Civil War—the Battle of Kennesaw Mountain. He grew up in Logansport and became a well-known judge.

How did he become such an important part of baseball history?

In 1919, several baseball players on the Chicago White Sox team were caught up in a scandal. The players were accused of taking bribes from gamblers in what came to be known as the "Black Sox Scandal."

The leaders of the sport began searching for someone who could restore order and honor to baseball. Eleven owners of baseball clubs asked Landis to become the sport's first commissioner. The Hoosier was given awesome powers—including the authority to impose any punishment he considered necessary on players or teams. One of Landis's first acts was to ban eight "Black Sox" players permanently from the sport.

In 1922, Landis even suspended Babe Ruth (the biggest star in baseball) and two other players for violating some rules. Some critics called Landis a "dictator." They said he was harder to approach than the president of the United States.

Fun fact: The "Black Sox Scandal" is the subject of the movie *Eight Men Out*. Much of the movie was filmed in Indianapolis in 1987. Landis is a major character in the film.

Marshall "Major" Taylor

One of the very first African-American athletes to become famous around the world was a Hoosier. But for several reasons, including bigotry in the late 1800s and early 1900s, Major Taylor had to leave his home state of Indiana—and, eventually, even the United States—to achieve great success.

His sport was bicycle racing, which was hugely popular in the days before most people owned cars. The real name of the athlete from Indianapolis was Marshall W. Taylor. Everyone called him "Major," though; he probably got the nickname at age thirteen when he worked at an Indianapolis bicycle shop. Talented young Taylor would perform bicycle tricks on sidewalks while wearing a military cap and a uniform with large brass buttons and braids, the kind of clothes worn by an Army major.

Major Taylor (1878–1932) had a dramatic life. He entered his first big bicycle race in secret because his friends were afraid that organizers would not let a black athlete compete in the event. Taylor, who was just sixteen, won that race in 1895—even though some people yelled racial slurs at him as he pedaled the seventy-five miles from downtown Indianapolis to

A family portrait in 1907 shows Major Taylor with his wife, Daisy, and their daughter, Sydney. (From the collection of Indiana State Museum and Historic Sites)

Major Taylor is shown here competing in a top bicycle race in Europe during the early 1900s. (From the collection of Indiana State Museum and Historic Sites)

the finish line in the small town of Matthews. A heavy rain began to fall during the race, forcing most of the other bicyclists to quit. Major Taylor not only won—he was the only bicyclist to even finish the race.

Many bicycle tracks in Indiana were open to whites only, though. So in 1896, just one year after winning the race to Matthews, Taylor left his home state and moved to Massachusetts. Soon he became a national, then a world, champion.

Even as Taylor was setting world records, he never was free from prejudice. In some cities on the racing circuit, he had to hunt to find places to eat and sleep. During races, gangs of white cyclists often worked together to try to force him to wreck or box him in.

In Europe, he found a little less bigotry. Bicycling also remained popular there in the early 1900s; in America, people began to lose interest as they focused on cars.

Taylor and his wife, Daisy, met the kings and queens of Europe. For a while, he enjoyed fabulous wealth and fame. In 1901, Taylor won forty-two out of fifty-seven races that he entered.

But the Hoosier athlete became exhausted. The vicious moves against him by other cyclists began to affect him, and he backed out of several races. Meanwhile, his advisers made bad decisions with his money. Daisy divorced him.

By the time he died, Major Taylor was living in poverty in Chicago. He had been forgotten. The once-great athlete was buried in a grave without a marker. The owner of the Schwinn Bicycle Company never forgot Mayor Taylor's heroics, though.

Several years after Taylor's death, Frank Schwinn organized a memorial service at the Chicago cemetery. Many famous athletes attended the ceremony, and a bronze marker was placed on Taylor's grave. It reads:

"World champion bicycle rider who came up the hard way without hatred in his heart. An honest, courageous and God-fearing, clean-living, gentlemanly athlete. A credit to his race who always gave out his best. Gone but not forgotten."

Did you know?

- Throughout his life, Major Taylor refused to race on Sundays. He explained that he had promised his mother "to lead an upright Christian life," and he thought Sundays should be saved for church and family. He lost thousands of dollars by refusing to compete in Sunday races.

- Marshall W. Taylor had a nickname besides "Major." The handsome, black bicyclist also was known as "The Ebony Streak" because of his speed.

- Fifty years after Taylor died, bicycling became popular again—and he was honored in his hometown. In 1982, a $2.5 million bicycle track was built in Indianapolis and named the Major Taylor Velodrome (pictured below). Considered one of the country's best racetracks, it seats as many as five thousand spectators around the cement track, which has twenty-eight-degree banking on the turns. Major national and world cycling races have been held at the velodrome. Record-breaking crowds for cycling attended the competitions for the 1987 Pan American Games and the 1982 National Sports Festival.

Photo by Stephen Baker

Football legends

Time out! Time out for football!

In 1984, the blue and white Indianapolis Colts came roaring to the newly built Hoosier Dome. (In 1994, the stadium was renamed the RCA Dome.) The Colts' first home base had been the city of Baltimore in Maryland. Before the team moved here, the Hoosier state did not have a major-league professional football team.

Even so, Indiana produced or was home of many famous football coaches and players. Some grew up in Indiana, and then played for pro teams in other states. Others were legendary coaches or players for spectacular football programs at Indiana's colleges.

Here is a look at the sport of football's biggest stars with strong links to Indiana:

Knute Rockne

The most distinguished college football team in the entire country may be the Fighting Irish of the University of Notre Dame in **South Bend**. In many seasons, the Fighting Irish are considered the Number One college team in the nation. The long record of football triumphs at Notre Dame was kicked off by an immigrant to America, a man who often is mentioned to this day as the most famous football coach in history. His name was **Knute Rockne**.

Have you ever heard the saying, "Go out there and win just one for the Gipper"?

It's probably the most famous phrase ever used to motivate athletes; according to legend, Coach Rockne first spoke it to his players in 1928. More about "the Gipper" in a bit. First, some background about Rockne.

He was born across the Atlantic Ocean in Voss, Norway, in 1888. Knute (pronounced like "newt") was five years old when his family came to America, settling in Chicago. Knute played football as a student at Notre Dame. (He was a member of the Class of 1913.) Then he stayed on campus to be a chemistry teacher and assistant football coach.

Rockne became head coach in 1918 and quickly enjoyed phenomenal success. During the 1920s, Notre Dame under Coach Rockne became the first college football team to travel all over the country for regular-season games. Also during the 1920s, four of Rockne's players in the backfield became famous with the nickname "The Four Horsemen." Coach Rockne also got a nickname: "The Rock."

His teams won six national championships. In five of Rockne's thirteen seasons as head coach, the Fighting Irish were unbeaten. Sadly, Coach Rockne's career was cut short. He was killed in 1931 when he was a passenger on a small airplane that crashed in Kansas.

Under "The Rock," the Fighting Irish built a huge fan base that remains loud and strong across the country to this day.

So what's the story behind the "win just one for the Gipper" phrase?

"Gipper" was yet another nickname. It's what Coach Rockne called one of his most popular players, handsome George Gipp. In 1920, while he was a student at Notre Dame, Gipper died of pneumonia. According to Rockne, Gipper made a deathbed request to the coach that "someday, when the going is real tough," the Fighting Irish should rally and win a game in his memory.

Eight years later, Notre Dame's team was playing only mediocre (average) football and lagging behind at halftime of a big game. To fire up his players in the locker room, Coach Rockne told them the story about the dying Gipper and his last wish. Inspired, the players returned to the football field to win the game.

Ara Parseghian

Another legendary football coach at the University of Notre Dame was **Ara Parseghian**. He coached the Fighting Irish from 1964 to 1975 and is credited with restoring the team to glory after a slump.

Like so many other coaches and players at Notre Dame, Parseghian had a nickname. His was "Hardnose." He earned the nickname because as a young player he would compete through pain—and because as a coach, he was tough.

Ara Parseghian was born in Akron, Ohio, in 1923. He grew up to play professional football; he was a halfback with the Cleveland Browns in the 1940s. But Parseghian's career as a player ended when he injured his hip in 1949.

His real fame came as the Notre Dame coach. Parseghian led the Fighting Irish to national championships in 1966 and 1973.

Since retiring, Parseghian has devoted much of his time to crusading on a health issue. He has been raising money to find a cure for a rare disease (called Niemann-Pick Disease Type C) that has stricken several of his grandchildren.

"As in most situations in my life, I won't accept this without a fight," Parseghian said during an interview in his office in South Bend. "We must find a cure."

Tom Harmon

In the late 1930s and '40s, good-looking **Tom Harmon** was one of the most famous football players in America.

Harmon (1919–1990) grew up in **Rensselaer** and **Gary** in northwestern Indiana. At Gary Mann High School, he was a football star and a state champion hurdler in track. Then, Harmon attended the University of Michigan, where he became a famous running back. As a Michigan player in 1940, Harmon won the Heisman Trophy, the highest award for a college player. (So far, Harmon is the only native Hoosier to win the Heisman.)

Harmon played one season of pro football before World War II interrupted his career. While he was serving in the Air Force, his plane was shot down over China. Harmon suffered serious burns on both legs and was awarded the Purple Heart. Even so, he managed to play two more seasons of pro football in the 1940s with the Los Angeles Rams. When his playing days were over, Harmon enjoyed a second successful career as a TV and radio sportscaster.

Bob Griese

Evansville native **Bob Griese** is in both the College Football Hall of Fame and the Professional Football Hall of Fame.

Griese, who was born in 1945, is in the college hall of fame because of his triumphs as a quarterback at Purdue University in the 1960s. He guided Purdue's team, the Boilermakers, to a thrilling victory in the Rose Bowl at the end of the 1966–1967 season. After graduating, Griese was drafted as a pro quarterback with the Miami Dolphins. He led the Dolphins to two Super Bowl championships in the 1970s.

Griese retired as a player after the 1980 season and became a TV analyst. He continues to live in Miami.

Jeff George

Early on, the Indianapolis Colts had a quarterback with hometown roots. **Jeff George** (born in 1967) first was in the national spotlight as a teenager when he demonstrated amazing ability as a quarterback at Warren Central High School in **Indianapolis**. In 1985 and 1986, young Jeff led the football team to back-to-back state championships and generally was considered the best high school quarterback in the nation.

He attended two colleges, playing as quarterback for teams at Purdue University and the University of Illinois.

In 1990, George returned to his hometown when the Indianapolis Colts made him the top pick in the National Football League draft. But his stay with the Colts was rocky. The team's management and many fans were upset when George held out from training camp over contract disputes. After four controversial seasons with the Colts, George left to become quarterback of the Atlanta Falcons.

Since then, he has played for the Oakland Raiders and the Washington Redskins. With the Redskins during the 2000–2001 season, George enjoyed the support of fans and his coaching staff that had eluded him with other teams. In Indiana, his total of 43 touchdowns in a single season (1985) still stands as a high school record.

Peyton Manning

Beginning with the 1998–1999 season, the Indianapolis Colts have been led by a hugely popular quarterback, personable **Peyton Manning.**

Like Jeff George several seasons earlier, Manning was the Number One pick in the NFL draft by the Colts. Unlike George, though, Manning is not a native of Indiana. He was born in 1976 in New Orleans, where his father, Archie Manning, was a star quarterback for the NFL's New Orleans Saints.

Growing up, Peyton memorized tapes of his dad's games. As a quarterback at the University of Tennessee, he smashed thirty-three different school regional or national records. (He also was an outstanding student, graduating "cum laude"—with honors.)

Manning's first year with the Colts was disappointing, ending with a 3–13 record. In the season that began in fall 1999, though, Peyton turned things around and took the Colts to the NFL playoffs. Peyton, who is six feet, five inches tall and weighs 230 pounds,

Knute Rockne, the legendary football coach who told the Fighting Irish to "win just one for the Gipper." (Courtesy of the University of Notre Dame)

Ara Parseghian, famous University of Notre Dame coach of the 1960s and '70s. (Courtesy of *The Indianapolis Star*)

Popular quarterback Peyton Manning of the Indianapolis Colts works out with his teammates in training camp. (Stephen Baker)

also was voted to be the starting quarterback in the Pro Bowl of 2000.

He quickly won praise from Hoosiers for his extensive work with hospitals, children's charities, and libraries. Manning also launched the PeyBack Classic, a football game in which five Indianapolis schools play in the RCA Dome. In 2000, Peyton and Archie Manning cowrote a book about football and family values.

Fun facts

- Knute Rockne's amazing record as head coach at the University of Notre Dame consisted of 105 wins, 12 losses, and 5 ties.

- The dying George Gipp was portrayed in a movie by an actor who went on to be president of the United States. Ronald Reagan played the Fighting Irish player in *Knute Rockne, All American*, a movie filmed on the Notre Dame campus in 1940.

- Ara Parseghian's record is second only to Rockne's as the coach with the most wins in Notre Dame football history. Parseghian's record consisted of 95 wins, 17 losses, and 4 ties.

- Famous running back Tom Harmon married a movie star of the 1940s. Her name was Elyse Knox. Their handsome son, Mark Harmon, is a popular actor who has starred in several movies and TV series.

- Another second-generation star (in this case, a *football* star) is the son of Bob Griese, Purdue University's onetime quarterback. Bob's son, Brian Griese, is a quarterback like his father. In the late 1990s, Brian Griese began playing for the Denver Broncos.

- When "hometown boy" Jeff George was drafted by the Indianapolis Colts in 1990, his $12 million contract made him the highest-paid rookie (first-year player) in the history of the National Football League to that point.

- In the book that Peyton Manning co-wrote with his father, he says: "I approach life on an order of four. First, my faith. Then, my family, my education and my athletics."

John Wooden

Many sports analysts consider **John Wooden** to be the best college basketball coach who ever lived. What's more, the influence of John Wooden—the first man named to the Basketball Hall of Fame as both a player and as a coach—stretches far beyond athletics.

John Robert Wooden, who was born in **Martinsville** in 1910, became hugely popular as a kindly, twinkle-eyed motivational speaker and source of folk wisdom. According to Coach Wooden, many of the morals and lessons that he has shared with thousands of audience members came from his nurturing, hard-working parents. John Wooden grew up on his family's sixty-acre farm near Martinsville; for many years, the Woodens' house had no electricity or indoor plumbing.

Young John faced the challenges of daily life by always carrying this motto written for him by his Hoosier father:

> *Be true to yourself. Make each day your masterpiece. Drink deeply from good books, especially the Bible. Make friendship a fine art. Build a shelter against a rainy day. Ask for guidance. And give thanks for your blessings each day.*

Wooden became an outstanding

In the 1940s, Johnny Wooden coached basketball at Indiana State University. Here he is in the locker room, giving his players a halftime pep talk during a national tournament. (Indiana State Museum and Historical Sites)

basketball player at Martinsville High School and Purdue University. His greatest glory—a remarkable streak of wins that accounts for his place as one of the greatest figures of twentieth century sports—occurred when he became the head basketball coach at the University of California at Los Angeles (UCLA). Before John Wooden arrived in 1948, the UCLA basketball team was the weakest in its conference.

Under Coach Wooden, UCLA teams won ten NCAA championships. (Seven of them—from 1967 through 1973—were in a row, a streak that probably never will be equaled.)

At one point, UCLA enjoyed a sensational series of eighty-eight straight wins. Some experts credit that with creating the annual basketball frenzy known as "March Madness."

When John Wooden retired as a coach in 1975, he stepped up his career as a motivational speaker. Thousands of Americans have used his "Pyramid for Success" plan. The "bricks" at the bottom of his pyramid are "Industriousness" and "Enthusiasm." The top of the pyramid is "Success." (In between are "Faith" and "Patience.")

"Do the best of which you are capable, and the score can never make you a loser," he tells audiences. "Do less than that and the score will not make you a winner."

Tony Hinkle

Basketballs are orange, right?

Well, not always. For many years, the balls were dark brown. It was the idea of a popular Indiana basketball coach to make basketballs orange.

That was one of many reasons Tony Hinkle of Butler University became a legendary figure. While he was at Butler, a small, private university in Indianapolis, Hinkle coached baseball and football as well as basketball—an awesome task. In the three sports, Coach Hinkle eventually chalked up a combined total of one thousand victories; he coached Butler's basketball team to a national championship in 1929.

Like John Wooden, Tony Hinkle was widely loved. Also like Coach Wooden, Tony Hinkle grew up on a farm. He was born Paul David Hinkle in 1898 on a farm near Logansport. A gifted athlete, he earned nine varsity letters at the University of Chicago. (Three letters each in basketball, football, and baseball.)

He came to Butler in 1921. For nearly fifty years, Tony Hinkle was a coach and teacher. In the late 1950s, Tony Hinkle crusaded to change the "muddy brown" color of basketballs. He wanted a brighter color so the ball would be easy to see in arenas, which were filling with ever-bigger crowds. The Spalding Company, which makes basketballs, worked with Coach Hinkle to produce the orange ball that became standard by the early 1960s. Also in the 1960s, the athletic arena on the Butler campus was renamed Hinkle Fieldhouse.

Tony Hinkle retired as a coach in 1970, but remained active in Butler affairs—and a popular figure on campus—for many more years. He died in 1992.

Bobby Knight

Love him or hate him—you can't ignore him.

Thousands of people have admired **Bobby Knight** for of his amazing success as Indiana University's basketball coach. He led the Hoosiers to three NCAA (National Collegiate Athletic Association) championships and eleven Big Ten championships. His fans also respect the fact that Knight ran a "clean" (no cheating) program during his twenty-nine years at IU and that almost all of his players went on to graduate. In addition, many fans respected Coach Knight's strict rules and stern manner of dealing with players—as well as his emphasis on team play rather than creating individual stars.

Many other people, though, objected to the famous coach's style. His hot temper and angry behavior toward players, administrators, and other people eventually cost Coach Knight his job. In September of 2000, IU President Myles Brand fired Knight for what he called a pattern of "defiant and hostile" behavior.

When he left **Bloomington**, Knight could point with pride to national championships in 1976, 1981, and 1987. He also coached American teams to gold medals at the 1984 Los Angeles

Flamboyant and often controversial basketball coach Bobby Knight. (Courtesy of *The Indianapolis Star*)

Olympics and the 1979 Pan American Games.

On the other hand, critics could point to one of his most unforgettable displays of temper—a chair-throwing incident. During a game against Purdue University in 1985, a referee gave Coach Knight a technical foul; Knight responded by picking up a chair and flinging it onto the playing floor. Eventually, officials ejected Knight from the game.

So what's the background of this colorful man, whose trademark became the bright red sweaters that he wore as IU coach from 1971 to 2000?

Bob Knight did not start life as a Hoosier. He was born in Ohio in the small town of Orrville. His mother, Hazel, was a teacher. His father, Carroll Knight (called "Pat"), was a railroad worker who took his job seriously.

"I remember him saying to me, 'If you are going to accept pay for something, do it right,'" Knight wrote years later. In high school, he played basketball, football, and baseball. Then he studied at Ohio State University and played on basketball teams that won three Big Ten championships.

Eventually, Knight became the head basketball coach at the U.S. Military Academy (Army) at West Point in New York. He has said that his stay at West Point gave him an appreciation for discipline—and, as he put it, "a way discipline could be applied to basketball and the players I would teach."

Under Knight, Army defeated its arch-rival Navy every year.

National attention focused on Bobby Knight almost instantly after the young coach arrived on the IU campus in 1971. He insisted on tough drills for his players—including having them run up the steps of Assembly Hall, the arena, before practice.

His teams in 1975 and 1976 became legendary. The '75 team was undefeated all season until losing to the University of Kentucky in the regional finals. The next year also ended with an undefeated regular season—and Knight's first NCAA championship.

Meanwhile, Coach Knight continued to draw attention—positive and negative. IU was fined several times for Knight's outbursts during games; for example, in 1987 the university was fined ten thousand dollars after Knight banged his fist on a scorer's table. Several players left IU over the years, blaming Knight's treatment of them. Yet Coach Knight also helped raise more than $5 million for the IU library. To many of his players, he was a hero.

The troubles that led to his firing began in early 2000 when Knight's boss, the IU athletic director, said he felt physically threatened by the coach. Then, a former player named Neil Reed claimed in a TV interview that Knight had grabbed him by the neck during a practice session in 1997; Knight contended he merely was moving Reed into position on the court.

After other accusations — including a secretary's statement that Knight got angry and threw a potted plant against a wall near her—the coach was placed on "zero tolerance" regarding any future outbursts.

Three months later, Knight argued with an IU student whom the coach claimed was being disrespectful. IU President Brand fired the coach, citing several incidents of what he called "unacceptable behavior," not just the clash with the student.

The day after his firing, Bob Knight bid farewell to Indiana at a rally attended by eight thousand supporters. In 2001, he was hired to coach the basketball team at Texas Tech University.

Did you know?

- Bobby Knight's record at IU was 661 wins, 240 losses. His overall record as a coach has been 763 wins, 290 losses.

- His full name is Robert Montgomery Knight.

- Coach Knight's wife, Karen, was a high school basketball coach in Oklahoma. Knight's first wife, Nancy, is the mother of his two sons, Tim and Patrick. Patrick played basketball for his father at IU from 1991 to 1995, and then became his dad's assistant coach.

- In an incident that drew a lot of publicity in 1987, IU had to forfeit (give up) a game to a team from the former Soviet Union because Coach Knight refused to leave the basketball floor after being ejected. (He had drawn three technical fouls for arguing with referees.) Later, when Knight was reprimanded by top IU administrators, at least as many people were angry with them as with the controversial coach.

Larry Bird

He called himself "the Hick from French Lick," but he went on to become known as "Larry Legend."

Many sports analysts consider **Larry Bird** from **French Lick**, Indiana, to be the greatest passing forward ever in the National Basketball Association and the most versatile player (one able to take on any role) in the history of the league.

Five years after retiring as a truly outstanding player for the Boston Celtics, "Larry Legend" returned to his home state to accept a new challenge. Beginning in 1997, Bird coached the Indiana Pacers for three successful years. (During the 1997–1998 season, the Pacers had fifty-eight victories, the most since the team joined the NBA in 1976.)

Yet this basketball superstar—a multimillionaire—once worked briefly as a garbage collector. So what's the story behind this unusual sports legend?

Larry Bird was born in 1956 and grew up in French Lick, a small town in southwestern Indiana. Before "Larry Legend," French Lick primarily was famous for a fancy hotel with health spas popular among wealthy people from all over the country.

The Birds were far from wealthy. In

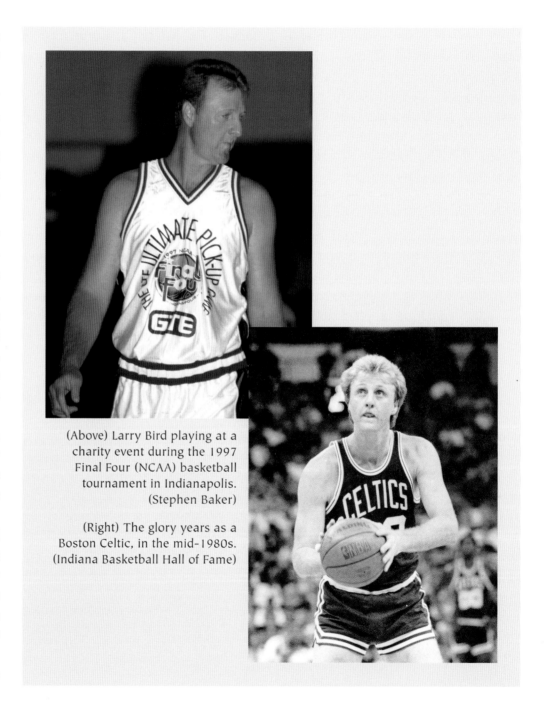

(Above) Larry Bird playing at a charity event during the 1997 Final Four (NCAA) basketball tournament in Indianapolis. (Stephen Baker)

(Right) The glory years as a Boston Celtic, in the mid-1980s. (Indiana Basketball Hall of Fame)

fact, the family was among the poorest in town. Larry, the fourth of six children in the family, became obsessed with basketball as a boy. He devoted almost every spare moment to perfecting his shooting skills.

"I played when I was cold and my body was aching and I was so tired," he recalled to *Sports Illustrated* magazine years later. "I don't know why. I just kept playing and playing . . . I guess I always wanted to make the most out of it."

At Springs Valley High School, Larry set nearly every record imaginable. After graduating in 1974, he won a coveted (widely desired) scholarship to play basketball at legendary Indiana University. After only a month, though, Larry dropped out and returned to French Lick. Years later, he explained that the big, sprawling IU campus—and the expensive clothes worn by some students—had overwhelmed him.

During this low period in French Lick, Larry grappled with several personal problems. He briefly was married to his high school sweetheart, but the couple divorced. His father died. As he struggled to pay bills, Bird worked as a garbage collector.

Then came the breakthrough for "the Hick from French Lick." Coaches at Indiana State University in Terre Haute had heard about Bird's amazing basketball ability and lured him with a scholarship. Bird, at six feet, nine inches tall and weighing 220 pounds,

Fun facts about Larry Bird

- His full name is Larry Joe Bird.

- He was the only living person—and the only athlete—to be named one of the "Ten Greatest Hoosiers of the 20th Century" by readers of *The Indianapolis Star*. In addition to choosing Larry Bird, thousands of readers of the state's largest newspaper voted for business leaders Eli Lilly III and Madam Walker, poet James Whitcomb Riley and composers Cole Porter and Hoagy Carmichael. Readers said they admired Larry Bird's modest attitude and hard work. So how did Larry react when told he had been named one of the Ten Greatest Hoosiers by thousands of newspaper readers? "I have no idea why they would do that," he said. It's an example of his modesty—and his dislike of being in the spotlight.

- Larry Bird played himself in a Hollywood movie called *Blue Chips* (1994). Portions of the movie (which is about—what else?—basketball) were filmed in Frankfort, Indiana.

- As pro players, Bird and "Magic" Johnson were praised for their unselfish play. They established a new style of team-oriented play that emphasized the pass.

- When Larry Bird was growing up in French Lick, his family was too poor to own a car. In his autobiography, Bird writes that his father tried to make the best of the situation when talking to the six children: "We lived near this big hill, and whenever I was going someplace, my dad would say, 'You know, Larry, if you run up that hill, you will get there faster.' . . . So I'd go out and run up that hill as fast as I could. Who needed a car?"

soon had all of America paying attention.

He averaged more than thirty points a game for two years. During one game with Indiana State's Sycamores, he scored forty-nine points. Bird began his junior year by being featured on *Sports Illustrated*'s cover as "Basketball's Secret Weapon."

The next season (1978–1979), Bird thrilled the campus of Indiana State by leading the Sycamore team to an undefeated regular season and a spot

in the NCAA finals. The Sycamores lost the championship to a team from Michigan State University led by Bird's career-long rival and friend, Earvin "Magic" Johnson.

After graduating from Indiana State with a degree in physical education, Bird was drafted by the Boston Celtics of the NBA. The man with blond bangs and a Hoosier twang signed a five-year contract reported at more than $3.25 million, making him the highest-paid rookie (first-year athlete) in the history of professional sports at the time.

Bird's impact on the Celtics was dramatic and immediate. He led the team to the greatest one-season turnaround (reversal from losses to wins) in NBA history; the Celtics went from a 29–53 record to 51–21 in Bird's first season.

Records started falling, and honors kept coming. In 1986, Bird was named *Sports Illustrated*'s "Sportsman of the Year." For three years in a row (1984–1986), he was named the NBA's most valuable player. Sports analysts credited Bird—and "Magic" Johnson, who now was playing for the Los Angeles Lakers—with lifting the NBA to new levels of athletic achievement and popularity with the public.

Some of Bird's stats as a pro player:

He led the NBA in free throw percentage four times and was elected to the NBA All-Star teams thirteen times. To top it off, he won an Olympic gold medal as a member (along with Magic Johnson) of America's legendary "Dream Team" during the Barcelona Olympic Games in 1992. In August of that year, Bird announced he was retiring as a Celtics player.

"It was one of the happiest moments of my life," he wrote in *Bird Watching*, his 1999 autobiography. That was because he had been playing with constant back pain for almost ten years. "No matter what I did—whether I was standing up, sitting down, lying down, leaning over—I couldn't escape it."

A golf lover, Bird and his second wife, Dinah, were living in Naples, Florida, and devoting a lot of time to charity when the offer to coach the Indiana Pacers came up in 1997. So Bird returned to Indiana, much to the delight of his fans. As a coach, he led the Pacers to the NBA's Eastern Conference finals for all three seasons. In his final season (1999–2000), the team even advanced to the NBA finals.

Bird was named to the Basketball Hall of Fame in 1998. When he retired as the Pacers' coach, he was replaced by Isiah Thomas.

Meanwhile, a street in French Lick was renamed. It's called Larry Bird Boulevard—and is located near the town's famous, lavish hotel.

Other basketball legends

Steve Alford

No wonder he became one of the most popular high school and college basketball players in Indiana history. Steve Alford of New Castle is polite, hard working, clean-cut, wholesome and modest.

Steve, who was born in 1965, never rebelled or lost his all-American image despite being coached by two of the most demanding masters of the game of basketball. One was his dad, Sam Alford, at New Castle High School (where Steve was named Indiana's "Mr. Basketball" in 1983). The other was Bobby Knight at Indiana University, which Steve led to an NCAA championship in 1987.

At IU, where Steve was a star shooting guard, he was named the team's "Player of the Year" each of his four years. He scored a total of 2,438 points over those years, one of the highest totals in the history of the Big Ten Conference.

Because his father was such a respected high school coach, Steve developed a love for basketball early—very early.

"For my first birthday, I got—what else?—my first basketball and hoop set," Steve wrote in his autobiography, *Playing for Knight* (1989).

In the book, Alford recalls his first look at the huge arena where his dad coached. New Castle Chrysler High School Fieldhouse, the country's largest high school gym, seats about ninety-five hundred people. Young Steve instantly vowed to fill it. He did, pairing with his dad to make an unstoppable player-coach combination.

Next, he played for Bob Knight at IU and on the United States team in the 1984 Summer Olympics; the Olympics team with Steve won a gold medal. When he led IU to the NCAA championship three years later, he became a hero to thousands of Hoosiers.

Steve played for four years in the NBA, and married his high school sweetheart, Tanya Frost.

Then he became a college coach, starting at Manchester College in North Manchester, Indiana. At his next college coaching jobs—Southwest Missouri State University (1995–1999) and the University of Iowa (where he's been since 1999)—he asked that he be able to hire a special person as his assistant coach: his dad, Sam Alford.

Many Hoosiers hope Steve Alford will return to IU as head coach someday. But in April of 2001, he extended his contract at Iowa for five years.

Damon Bailey

When he was only a junior high student in tiny Heltonville, Indiana, Damon Bailey found himself in the national spotlight.

That's because Damon, a southern Indiana farm boy, was watched in his junior high basketball games by famous Indiana University coach Bobby Knight. Coach Knight praised young Damon to the author of a best-selling book, *A Season on the Brink* (1987). The author, John Feinstein, described Damon's talents in his book.

Damon, who was born in 1971, would go on to play outstanding basketball for Coach Knight. First, though, he led Bedford-North Lawrence High School to four straight appearances in the "Final Four" of the state tourney. Because Damon was just as clean-cut and hard-working as Steve Alford had been before him, the fan frenzy he created was so intense that it got a special name: "Damon-mania."

In his high school senior year of 1990, Damon Bailey and his Bedford-North Lawrence teammates won the state championship. Damon also became the leading scorer in Indiana high school history.

Next came four years playing for Coach Knight and the Cream and Crimson at IU. Although his IU teams never won an NCAA championship or even advanced to college basketball's "Final Four," Damon enjoyed several successes. In his junior year of 1993, the IU team won seventeen Big Ten games—the most for the Hoosiers in more than fifteen years. During his days at IU, Damon received tremendous public sympathy when it was learned that his sister, Courtney, was battling leukemia.

She recovered, and Damon married his longtime girlfriend, Stacey Ikerd, a former Bedford-North Lawrence cheerleader. Damon had surgery on both knees, then played pro basketball briefly in Fort Wayne and overseas in France.

George McGinnis

In 1969, many sports experts considered **George McGinnis** of **Indianapolis** the best high school athlete in the country.

That was the year that George McGinnis, a power forward, led Washington High School to an unbeaten season and a state championship. His amazing thirty-five points during the

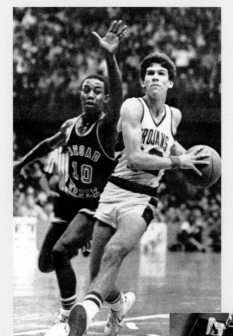

Steve Alford drives for a clear shot for New Castle High School in the semistate game of the 1983 state tournament. During this game against Broad Ripple High School of Indianapolis, Alford scored fifty-seven points. (Indiana Basketball Hall of Fame)

Damon Bailey (center) celebrated after his Bedford-North Lawrence High School team won the state championship in 1990, his senior year of high school. (Indiana Basketball Hall of Fame)

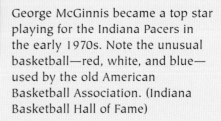

George McGinnis became a top star playing for the Indiana Pacers in the early 1970s. Note the unusual basketball—red, white, and blue—used by the old American Basketball Association. (Indiana Basketball Hall of Fame)

championship game instantly became part of "Hoosier Hysteria" folklore. He set a state tourney record that still stands by scoring 148 points in the final four games.

Named the state's "Mr. Basketball" in 1969, he went on to triumphs at Indiana University. In his second year on campus, George led the Big Ten in scoring and rebounding; he was the first sophomore in the league's history to do so.

Then George, who was born in 1950, became one of the outstanding pro players of the 1970s. "Big Mac," who is six feet, eight inches tall, led the Indiana Pacers (then part of the American Basketball Association) to two league titles. He also played for the Philadelphia 76ers.

Since retiring as a player in the early 1980s, "Big Mac" has remained in the public eye. He is an Indianapolis-based businessman and a TV and radio sportscaster.

Bobby Plump

Have you heard Hoosiers talk about the "Milan Miracle"?

Milan is a tiny town in Ripley County in southeastern Indiana. In 1954, Milan High School was one of the smallest schools in the state, with a senior class of only twenty-seven students.

One of them was Bobby Plump, whose life was forever changed by "the shot."

It was a stunning, fifteen-foot jump shot that he scored—just before the buzzer sounded!—against the seemingly much more powerful team from Muncie Central High School. So in the 1954 state championship, little "David" slew the mighty "Goliath" of Indiana high school basketball.

The unexpected victory of the "Mighty Men of Milan"—Bobby Plump and his teammates—inspired the movie *Hoosiers* (1986). It also became the most famous single event in "Hoosier Hysteria."

Bobby Plump, who was born in 1936, actually grew up in Pierceville, a town even smaller than nearby Milan. It was so small that it didn't have a high school. According to town folklore, Bobby Plump and his friends would play barnyard basketball until the

darkness of midnight by hanging a light bulb from a shovel handle.

At Milan High School, Bobby (who is five feet, ten inches tall) and his teammates became known as the small team with the big heart. The team—which included Ray Craft, Ron Truitt, Gene White, and Roger Schroder—was coached by a new teacher named Marvin Wood.

In the "Milan Miracle" state championship game of 1954, the final score—after Bobby's last-second jump shot—was Milan 32, Muncie Central 30.

The "Milan Miracle" probably won't be repeated by another small-town team. In 1998, a new tournament system was introduced. High schools across Indiana are divided into four classes based on their size. That means at the end of the tourney, there are four "class" champions.

Bobby Plump eventually became the owner of a restaurant in the Broad Ripple area of Indianapolis. It's called Plump's Last Shot.

Reggie Miller

At Conseco Fieldhouse in March of 2001, **Reggie Miller** made the two thousandth three-point shot of his professional career. When the ball went through the basketball net, Miller set an all-time record for "three-pointers" in the National Basketball Association.

Long before that historic jump shot, though, Reggie Miller had become the first genuine superstar of the Indiana Pacers. Thanks largely to lanky, popular Miller, the state of Indiana (long known for "Hoosier Hysteria" because of high school and college basketball) finally became a state of pro basketball fans.

Miller (who was born in 1965) grew up in California, but has adopted **Indianapolis** as his hometown. The Indiana Pacers guard, who wears Number 31, has spent his entire pro career with the team—fourteen seasons and counting. Along the way, Reggie became a five-time NBA All-Star.

In 1994—as thousands of fans chanted "Reg-gie! Reg-gie! Reg-gie!"— he led the team to its first victories in the second round of the NBA playoffs. The 1999-2000 season was even more exciting: Reggie led the Pacers to the

Reggie Miller, basketball superstar (Courtesy of *The Indianapolis Star*)

NBA Finals. (The team eventually lost to the Los Angeles Lakers in six games.)

Reggie, who is six feet, seven inches tall and weighs 195 pounds, makes it look easy to play basketball. But all of his success (he's expected to be voted in the Basketball Hall of Fame one day) didn't come easily or quickly.

Reggie was born with a handicap called "pronated hip." His leg bones forced his ankles inward. Doctors told Miller's parents that he might never walk unassisted, let alone play basketball. He wore steel braces at night until he was four years old. After that, Reggie wore corrective shoes. His mother, Carrie Miller, used to wake young Reggie once an hour through the night to turn him so his leg bones would rotate.

But Miller says he has mostly positive memories of his boyhood in a suburban city near Los Angeles. He was the fourth of five children, and he says he loved growing up in a large, close-knit family.

"There was always someone who had gone through the same thing," he says. "I didn't feel really alone."

Reggie wasn't even the first superstar in the Miller household. His sister Cheryl is regarded by many experts as the best women's basketball player ever. Cheryl Miller (who is one year older than Reggie) led the U.S. women's team to an Olympic gold medal in 1984. Reggie also won an Olympic gold medal. He was a key member of Dream Team III, a squad of NBA superstars that won gold at the 1996 Olympics in Atlanta.

He first tasted national stardom in college; Miller was an outstanding guard on UCLA's team. When he graduated in 1987, the Indiana Pacers made him their Number-One draft pick.

Reggie Miller took Indiana—and the country—by storm. He has endorsed everything from Nike shoes to McDonald's hamburgers and Marsh supermarkets.

In 1992, he married a fashion model, Marita Stavrou. (The couple divorced in 2001.) He has appeared on dozens of national talk shows such as *The Tonight Show With Jay Leno*.

Through it all, Miller hardly ever gives up or rests. Consider this statistic: As of more than midway through the 2000–2001 season, the Pacers had played a total of 1,139 games during "the Reggie years." Reggie played in all but twenty-six of those games.

Women sports stars from Indiana

Anita DeFrantz

She wasn't an athlete when she attended Shortridge High School in Indianapolis during the late 1960s and early seventies. That's because, unless you count cheerleading, there were no organized sports for girls at Shortridge—or at most high schools.

Yet Anita DeFrantz (1952–) has gone on to become, as *The Sporting News* put it in 1996, "the most powerful woman in sports." She is vice president of the International Olympic Committee (IOC), the worldwide organization that oversees the Olympics. In early 2001, DeFrantz announced plans to run for IOC president—which would make her the first woman and the first black in the top job.

Her initial fame came when she won the bronze medal in rowing at the 1976 Montreal Olympics. DeFrantz, who is five feet, eleven inches tall and powerfully built, took up rowing in college after graduating from Shortridge. For the 1984 Los Angeles Olympics, she managed the athletes' village—the small city where thousands of men and women live while competing in the Games.

As the highest-ranking woman on the IOC board, she used her clout to have the 1996 Summer Olympics in

Anita DeFrantz, often called "the most powerful woman in sports." (United States Olympic Committee)

Atlanta and the 2002 Winter Games in Salt Lake City.

"As I travel around the world, I speak of myself as 'the kid from Indianapolis,'" she said in a 1998 interview. "Who would have thought I'd be shaking hands with the mayor of Moscow?"

DeFrantz spent several years crusading for the inclusion of women's softball as an Olympic sport. When softball finally debuted during the 1996 Atlanta Olympics, the International Softball Federation gave her a medal of honor as a gesture of thanks.

Jaycie Phelps

In what sport can you win a gold medal if you only are five feet tall, weigh ninety-seven pounds, and are sixteen years old? Gymnastics.

Jaycie Phelps of Greenfield won a gold medal in team gymnastics at the 1996 Atlanta Olympics. She was a member of the famous "Magnificent Seven" group of athletes who captured America's first gold medal for women's team gymnastics.

The road to Phelps' victory was rough for her family. When she was in her early teens, Jaycie Phelps (born in 1979) moved from Greenfield to Arizona, then to Cincinnati, Ohio, in search of better coaching. Her father and brother usually remained in Greenfield and visited on weekends. All of the hardship and hard work paid off, though, when Phelps and her "Mag-

nificent Seven" teammates stunned the world by competing through injuries. (Phelps' teammate, Kerri Strug, had to be carried to the gold medal podium because she had sprained her ankle during competition.)

After knee surgery, Phelps worked to launch a comeback for the 2000 Sydney Olympics. Unfortunately, she was unable to make the American team.

Lindsay Benko

In her hometown of Elkhart, Lindsay Benko started swimming at a country club at age six. She grew up to win a gold medal in a freestyle swimming relay at the 2000 Summer Olympics in Sydney, Australia.

Lindsay was a state champion swimmer as a high school student in Elkhart. She followed that up with a spectacular college swimming career at the University of Southern California.

"The Number One priority for me is having fun," Lindsay (who was born in 1976) has written. "If I'm not having a good time, it's not worth it. I always want to make sure in workouts or at swim meets that I'm having fun."

She added, "When I sign autographs, I write, 'Follow your dreams,' because dreams make anything possible."

Jaycie Phelps of Greenfield (right) won a gold medal as a member of the "Magnificent Seven" women's gymnastics team in the 1996 Atlanta Olympics. (Stephen Baker)

Other sports with Hoosier stars

Bowling

Two men from Indiana dominated the world of professional bowling in different eras.

Richard "Dick" Weber of Indianapolis was the top bowler of the 1960s. Weber (born in 1929) started bowling at age ten at a bowling center that his dad managed. The Professional Bowling Association named him "Player of the Year" in 1961, 1963, and 1965.

During the 1980s, Mike Aulby of Indianapolis was the best pro bowler in the country. Aulby (born in 1960) graduated from Franklin Central High School and went on to be the top moneymaker on the pro bowling tour in 1985 and 1989. Today, Aulby lives in Carmel and serves as his sport's goodwill ambassador to several charities, including the Children's Miracle Network. Aulby was inducted into the PBA Hall of Fame in 1996.

Figure skating

Worldwide attention fell on Marion, Indiana, during the 1988 Winter Olympics because of clean-cut Wayne and Natalie "Kim" Seybold. The brother-sister pairs team of figure skaters over-came injuries and financial hardships to compete in the Olympics.

The young Seybolds (Wayne was born in 1963, Kim in 1965) lived with their parents in a small trailer for most of their years of training so there would be enough money to pay their coaches. Thanks to donations from Marion residents and businesses, Wayne and Kim were able to pursue their Olympic dreams.

The Seybolds finished tenth at the Calgary Olympics in 1988, and then toured as professional skaters. In 1995, Kim successfully recovered from surgery for a brain tumor.

Golf

The most famous golfer from Indiana, Fuzzy Zoeller of New Albany, has won two of the world's major golf tournaments: the Masters championship in 1979 and the U.S. Open in 1984. Zoeller was born in 1951; his real name is Frank Urban Zoeller.

He is a colorful character who is known for whistling around golf courses no matter how poorly he is playing.

Gymnastics

Kurt Thomas (born in 1956) became the first truly great American male gymnast while attending Indiana State University in the 1970s. Before Kurt won the world championship in 1978, Russians and Ukrainians dominated men's gymnastics.

In 1979, Thomas won the Sullivan Award as the country's top amateur athlete. In his trademark routine on the pommel horse and floor exercise, Kurt flared his legs in a flashy series of whirling, alternating, midair scissors kicks. The move is called the "Thomas Flare" to this day.

Horse racing

The best athlete in any sport during the early 1900s was a Hoosier, but he was not a human being. Dan Patch (born in 1896) was a harness racing horse, or trotter.

As a colt in the town of Oxford, Indiana, Dan Patch was ridiculed because he was gangly, or skinny. Beginning in 1900, though, "The Patch" had an incredible string of wins. His dominance on the grand circuit hurt

Don't try this at home: Gymnast Kurt Thomas does a handstand on the top step of the RCA Dome (then called the Hoosier Dome) in 1990. Thomas, the first truly great American male gymnast and then in his thirties, was attempting to make a comeback. (Courtesy of *The Indianapolis Star*)

Famous racehorse Dan Patch inspired a dance called "The Dan Patch Two-Step"; the sheet music is shown here. The unbeatable horse endorsed everything from sleds to dog food. (Indiana Historical Society)

betting at racetracks because everyone knew which horse would win. Dan Mesner, his Indiana owner, eventually became so nervous that a rival owner might poison Dan Patch, he sold him.

As a national celebrity, Dan Patch endorsed everything from dog food to sleds and washtubs. In 1916, both Dan Patch and his last owner (a Minneapolis businessman) were stricken with heart failure. The horse died July 11; his owner passed away the next day.

Swimming

The most famous athlete and the most famous coach in swimming history both have strong ties to Indiana University in **Bloomington**.

Mark Spitz (born in 1950) won an incredible seven gold medals at the 1972 Summer Olympics. With each of those seven victories, he set a world record. That's a feat many consider the most outstanding achievement in Olympic history in any sport.

Handsome, dark-haired Mark Spitz grew up in California, but was living in Bloomington as an IU student during the years of his history-making accomplishments. He was particularly known for his talent with the butterfly stroke, one of swimming's most difficult events.

His coach at IU was the legendary **James "Doc" Counsilman**, often considered the world's best swimming coach.

Wayne and Natalie "Kim" Seybold demonstrate their Olympic form. (Courtesy of Kim Seybold Catron)

The Seybolds on their return from the 1988 Olympics to their hometown of Marion, Indiana. Marion residents and businesses rallied around the pair and helped fund their Olympic dream. (Courtesy of Kim Seybold Catron)

Swimmer Mark Spitz poses with his record-breaking seven gold medals at the 1972 Summer Olympics. (Photofest)

Doc (born in 1920) coached forty-seven other Olympians besides Spitz. He was credited with "reinventing" the sport by applying scientific theories to analyze and improve swimming strokes. For decades, he designed training equipment used around the world and coached other swimmers.

In 1979, though, Doc Counsilman set a record of his own. At the age of fifty-eight, he became the oldest person to swim the English Channel.

The Andretti family

Around the world, the name of one family—"the Andrettis"—is associated more than any other with the Indianapolis 500, high speeds and racing charisma. Although several members of the Italian-American family have slid behind the wheel on various racing circuits, three Andrettis in particular have distinguished themselves.

They are **Mario Andretti,** winner of the 1969 Indianapolis 500 and a superstar of racing; his son, **Michael Andretti,** who was "Rookie of the Year" at the Indianapolis Motor Speedway in 1984; and Mario's nephew, **John Andretti,** who drew worldwide attention in May of 1994.

That's when John became the first race driver in history to compete in the 500-Mile Race and another major race—six hundred miles away—on the very same day. He raced in the 500 in the morning, then hopped aboard a helicopter at the Speedway, which took him to a private jet; that flew him to North Carolina, where John competed in the late afternoon in the NASCAR Coca-Cola 600 stock car race. Whenever John Andretti, who was born in 1963, races at the Speedway, he is viewed as a hometown favorite. The witty, personable race car driver grew up in the **Indianapolis** area and grad-

Mario Andretti, superstar race driver and "honorary Hoosier." (Courtesy of *The Indianapolis Star*)

Indianapolis businessman Aldo Andretti, Mario's identical twin brother, quit racing after two serious accidents. Behind Aldo is a photo of the racing Andrettis (from left): Jeff, John, Michael, and Mario. (Courtesy of *The Indianapolis Star*)

uated from Ritter High School on the city's west side, not far from the Speedway. At Ritter, John met his future wife, Nancy.

Since the 1980s John Andretti has driven on several racing circuits—and even competed in two different types of races (the Indianapolis 500 and the Brickyard 400) at the Speedway. John has competed in seven 500s, capturing the "Rookie of the Year" award in 1988, four years after his cousin Michael. He won his first Indy car (open-wheel car, the type that race at the Indy 500) race in Australia in 1991. That same year, John Andretti finished fifth at the 500.

In stock car racing, John often gives two other drivers with Hoosier connections a run for their money: Jeff Gordon and Tony Stewart. John reg-ularly races in the Brickyard 400 and finished a personal best of seventh in 1998. A year earlier, John won one of NASCAR's biggest races at the Daytona International Speedway in Florida. Despite his successes, John Andretti has one major regret.

"My biggest wish is that my dad could be racing with me," he said in a 1994 interview. "I think I got cheated."

His dad, Aldo Andretti, is Mario's identical twin brother. The twins were born in a little town in Italy in 1940 during World War II. As young boys, they shared a toy truck that they took turns playing with. Then they shared a bicycle. When Mario and Aldo Andretti were fifteen, they moved to America with their parents. The twins began auto racing—sharing one car. Mario would race in the car one week, Aldo the next.

But then Aldo (whom many, including Mario, considered the better driver) barely survived two horrible accidents. He quit racing and became an Indianapolis businessman while Mario went on to become a true superstar of Indy car racing.

Mario and his oldest son Michael (who was born in 1962) have lived most of their lives in Pennsylvania. But both have said they consider Indianapolis a "second home."

Handsome, colorful Mario Andretti has been linked to the Hoosier state ever since his first Indy car victory; it was at Indianapolis Raceway Park in 1965. That same year, he qualified for

John Andretti gets a hug from his mother, Corky, in 1988 at the Indianapolis Motor Speedway. (Courtesy of *The Indianapolis Star*)

his first 500, impressed experts by finishing third and was named "Rookie of the Year."

In addition to winning the 500 in 1969, Mario came close to capturing victory several other times at the Speedway over the next twenty-five years. During that period, he won championships on other racing circuits, including stock cars (Mario won NASCAR's Daytona 500 in 1967) and Formula One races on regular road tracks overseas in Europe.

Mario Andretti is the only person ever named "Driver of the Year" in three different decades: 1967, 1978, and 1984. A fan favorite, Mario was the subject of countless tributes during his "Farewell, Mario" retirement tour in 1994. His biggest frustration was never winning a second 500.

Other race car drivers from Indiana

Increasingly, more drivers in "the greatest spectacle in racing" are choosing to live in the Indianapolis area all year, not just during the month of May. For example, popular Scott Sharp, the pole sitter for the Indianapolis 500 in 2001, has moved to Carmel, Indiana, from the state of Connecticut, where he grew up.

Several fan favorites among the 500-Mile Race drivers of the past were even more thoroughly Hoosier. Wilbur Shaw (1902–1954) of Shelbyville, Indiana, dominated the Indianapolis 500 for several years. Shaw won the 500 three times—in 1937, 1939, and 1940. Those last two victories made him the first driver to earn back-to-back wins. He finished second in three other 500-Mile Races.

As a youth, Shaw had been an errand boy in Gasoline Alley at the Speedway. Many experts credit him with helping save the famous racetrack in the 1940s when, as a champion driver, Shaw persuaded Terre Haute businessman Tony Hulman to buy the Indianapolis Motor Speedway. It had been deteriorating during World War II, and, at Shaw's urging, Hulman pumped thousands of dollars into the track and restored its grandeur.

Wilbur Shaw was not always lucky. He almost won a fourth 500 victory: Shaw was in the lead in 1941 when a wheel hub broke on his car. The car slammed into the wall, and Shaw injured his back. Fifteen years later, Shaw was killed in a plane crash in northern Indiana.

A tragic plane crash also took the life of a driver in a well-liked family of professional racers. The Bettenhausens have experienced several tragedies, most recently a plane crash in the winter of 2000 that killed former race driver Tony Bettenhausen Jr. and his wife. Tony Jr., who was born in 1951, raced in eleven Indianapolis 500s. His best finish was in 1981, his rookie year, when Tony Jr. finished seventh.

His older brother, Gary Bettenhausen, had been one of the most active race drivers of the 1960s and '70s. Gary, who was born in 1941 and lives in Monrovia, Indiana, was known as a fierce competitor on the racetrack. Even so, he drew praise for his compassion during a race in 1971 when he stopped to help Mike Moseley, a rival driver. Moseley was pinned in a burning car, and Gary Bettenhausen helped him escape.

In 1972 Gary nearly won the Indianapolis 500; he was enjoying a comfortable lead when he was forced out with ignition problems just eighteen laps before the checkered flag. Two years later, he suffered serious injuries to his right arm during a dirt track race.

Gary and Tony Bettenhausen Jr. drove in their final Indy 500 (as teammates) in 1993. That was seven years before Tony was killed in the crash of the plane that he was piloting. By then, he had become the owner of a racing team based in Indianapolis.

The brothers' father, Tony Bettenhausen Sr., also had been a famous race driver. Tony Sr. (1916–1961) had a streak of bad luck at the Speedway. In his rookie Indianapolis 500 in 1946, he was forced out by mechanical problems with his car. That kind of thing became a pattern at the Speedway for Tony Sr. Although he won many races elsewhere, he didn't finish a 500-Mile Race until 1958, when he captured fourth place.

Tony Sr. finished fourth at the 500 the next year as well, but then came the first family tragedy. A couple of weeks before the Indianapolis 500 of 1961, Tony Sr. agreed to test-drive the car of a fellow driver and suggest improvements. The car crashed at the Speedway, and Tony Sr. was killed.

By the time Mario retired, Michael Andretti had roared his way to wins on various racing circuits and had some frustrations just as his father did. In the 500 Mile Race, Michael finished second in 1991. The next year, he dominated the 500 and led 160 of the 200 laps—but suddenly struggled with car problems and ended up thirteenth.

Michael Andretti stayed away from the Speedway for six years—from 1995 through 2000—because of a feud between two racing leagues. They are CART (Championship Auto Racing Teams, Michael's league) and the IRL (Indy Racing League), which competed at the Speedway. During those years, Michael won forty CART races—a record number—around the world.

In 2001, Michael Andretti thrilled Hoosier fans by returning to the Speedway to race in the 500. He has an unusual record in the Indianapolis 500. Over the years, Michael has led the race more laps (382) than any other driver who has never won it.

It's a distinction—part honor, part frustration—that symbolizes his family's up-and-down relationship with the Speedway. The dramatic twists and turns also are a reason that the colorful Andrettis have fascinated the four hundred thousand fans on race day at the Speedway for nearly forty years.

Legends in Business
and Science

The Studebaker brothers

Several states claim to be the birthplace of the automobile. Indiana is one of them—thanks to an inventor named **Elwood Haynes** who lived in **Kokomo** for much of his life. Haynes (1857–1925) began work on developing cars as early as 1891. His automobile factory in Kokomo was considered to have been the oldest in the United States. It made cars until the early 1920s, but was too small to survive. Cars had become so popular by then that other auto factories were growing quicker and became much bigger.

One of the biggest automakers—in fact, the biggest business in the city of **South Bend** for many, many years—was begun by five brothers. The Studebaker brothers not only worked together, they looked a lot alike. All of them had long, flowing beards and serious faces.

Beginning in the 1850s, the Studebakers made wagons. Eventually, they also made fancy carriages and buggies (the kind pulled by horses) that were sold all over the country. Then in the early 1900s, factories owned by the Studebakers started making cars. They were a tremendous success. Many of the Studebaker cars were flashy-looking and expensive. Some were convertibles.

The five Studebaker brothers (From left): Clement, Peter, Henry, F. Jacob, and John Mohler. The youngest brother, Jacob, was the least involved in the family business. He joined Studebaker Brothers in the late 1860s and died in 1887. (Courtesy of The Studebaker National Museum, South Bend, Indiana)

The copy in this 1950 advertisement for the Commander convertible described it as the "top of the line" car for Studebaker that year. (Courtesy of The Studebaker National Museum, South Bend, Indiana)

The five Studebaker brothers were, in order of age: Henry, Clement, John Mohler (known as "J. M." or "Wheelbarrow Johnny"), Peter, and Jacob.

Their father, John Clement Studebaker, was a hard-working blacksmith in South Bend. He often told his sons: "Boys, you must all learn a trade."

So in 1852, with just sixty-eight dollars, Henry (born in 1826) and Clement (born in 1831) opened a blacksmith shop.

How did their fortune get started?

Thanks go to J. M. (born in 1833). About the time that his older brothers were opening the blacksmith shop, nineteen-year-old J. M. built a wagon and used it to leave South Bend. He traveled to California as part of the famous Gold Rush. Beginning a few years earlier in 1849, thousands of people from the East and Midwest flocked to California because miners had discovered gold there.

But when J. M. Studebaker showed up at the mining camps in 1853, he had a better idea than wasting his time hunting for gold. (After all, he reasoned, how could he find gold when hundreds of other men also were searching for it everywhere?)

Instead, he asked himself, "What can I sell to all of these miners?"

The answer: wheelbarrows. Clearly, every miner needed a wheelbarrow to haul his gold and his supplies. J. M., as the son of a wagon-maker and blacksmith, knew how to make them. That's how he became known as "Wheelbarrow Johnny." Demand for his wheelbarrows was so intense at the mining camps that he earned ten dollars for each wheelbarrow, a huge amount in those days.

By the time J. M. returned to South Bend in the late 1850s, he was rich. He invested his money in his brothers' wagon-making operation, and business boomed. During the Civil War, the Studebaker brothers supplied wagons for the Union Army. After the war, business continued to boom because Americans needed wagons as they moved west—and Studebaker Brothers' wagons had a reputation for quality.

The brothers became famous around the world. Clement was a friend of three American presidents, including Benjamin Harrison from Indiana. Not even two horrible fires at the Studebakers' operations—in 1872 and 1874—ruined the brothers. After each fire, they simply rebuilt and made more wagons.

The Studebakers built their first car

What do spiffy cars cost today?

Sixty-year-old cars (and even older ones!), including those made by the Studebakers, often sell for a lot of money when they are polished and tuned up to their original condition—that is, restored.

People who love vintage (old) automobiles sometimes pay thousands of dollars more to buy one of them today than they would have had to pay when the car was made. That's particularly the case when the car is hard to find because so few remain in the world—such as the President roadster made by the Studebakers.

According to Andy Beckman, curator of collections at the Studebaker National Museum in South Bend, a two-door President roadster (which is an open car, or convertible) from 1931 sells for fifty thousand to sixty thousand dollars. When the President roadster was new in 1931, it sold for only $1,950. There are only fifty-seven President roadsters left in the world.

Also in 1931, the Studebakers manufactured a President coupe. (Unlike a roadster, a coupe has a top.) One of them is on display at the Studebaker National Museum; they sell for slightly less money than the roadster.

"There's a saying, 'When the top goes on, the price goes down,' " Beckman says. In other words, fancy convertibles often are more expensive than cars with roofs; many people consider old convertibles particularly cool-looking.

A Commander convertible from 1950, which also was made by the Studebakers, sold for $2,328 when it was introduced. The Commanders (which are bullet-nosed and have two doors) now sell for $18,000 to $20,000.

The Commanders were considered Studebakers' "top of the line"—that is, their best car—when they were made in the early 1950s. There are fewer than one hundred Commander convertibles left.

in 1902. Sadly, not all of the brothers lived to see the automobile age. The two youngest brothers died first: Jacob in 1887 and Peter in 1897.

For years after the brothers died— Clement passed away in 1901 and Wheelbarrow Johnny in 1915—their business continued making cars. The South Bend plant finally closed in 1963, more than a hundred years after Henry and Clement had started it all— with sixty-eight dollars and a dream.

The Ball brothers

The Studebakers from South Bend weren't the only Hoosier brothers to create a booming business famous across the country. The Ball brothers in Muncie also were fabulously successful. For decades and decades beginning in the 1880s, the Ball name was on clear, glass jars used by American families for canning vegetables and fruits. (Fresh fruit is canned so it can be saved and eaten in winter or other seasons.)

Just as there were five Studebaker brothers, there were five Ball brothers. They were, in order of age: Lucius, William C., Edmund Burke, Frank, and George.

Their father, Lucius Stiles Ball, was a farmer in Ohio, where the boys were born. When the brothers were teenagers, the Ball family moved to upstate New York. That's where two of the brothers—Edmund (1855–1925) and Frank (1857–1943)—opened a small factory that made tin oil cans. By 1884, Edmund and Frank were making glass fruit jars and had been joined by their other brothers.

The Balls came to Muncie in 1886 because the city offered them seven acres and five thousand dollars in moving expenses. Their factory opened in 1888 and achieved astounding success, particularly with its glass Mason jars.

The brothers used their wealth and influence to benefit Muncie in many ways. The eldest Ball brother, Lucius (1850–1932), became a doctor in Muncie. The brothers funded Ball Memorial Hospital and developed the college now known as Ball State University.

The famous Ball brothers of Muncie, Indiana: (from left) George A., Lucius L., Frank C., Edmund B., and William C.

Colonel Eli Lilly

Eli Lilly and Company is a $6 billion company based in Indianapolis that makes medicine sold around the world. But this giant company once was practically a one-man shop; it began as a small business that opened May 10, 1876, on a side street that really was no more than an alley.

The owner was a thirty-seven year-old chemist and Civil War hero named **Colonel Eli Lilly.** This ambitious Hoosier already had failed at several efforts, including an attempt to run a cotton plantation in the deep South. But Colonel Lilly didn't give up—and he was an "idea man." From the day he opened his humble business in the alley known as Pearl Street (the only words on his sign were: "Eli Lilly, Chemist"), he dreamed that his shop would become a major drug company.

Lilly (1838–1898) grew up in Greencastle. He studied pharmacy (the making of drugs and medicine) before the outbreak of the Civil War. During the war, Lilly organized the Indiana Light Artillery Brigade; it eventually became part of a famous fighting unit known as "the Lightning Brigade."

Eventually, Lilly was captured by the Confederates and thrown in prison. But he was released and, by the end of the Civil War in 1865, had been promoted to the rank of colonel.

Colonel Eli Lilly: Civil War hero, chemist and civic leader. (Courtesy of Eli Lilly and Company Archives)

After the war, he stayed in the South and bought a cotton plantation of twelve hundred acres. A drought in Mississippi caused the cotton crop to fail. Then came a worse development, a family tragedy. In 1860, Colonel Lilly's young wife, Emily, died of a massive illness, probably malaria. Nearly overcome with grief, the colonel was left alone to care for the couple's five-year-old son, Josiah Kirby (later known as "J. K.") Lilly.

"The bright and joyous bride I led to the altar under your roof is gone," Lilly wrote to his family members in

Indiana. "My precious Emily, who you loved so dearly, is no more."

Within a few years, the Colonel decided he should return to the North and start a chemical business. He remarried and eventually moved with his new family to Indianapolis. The shop on Pearl Street sold medicine, syrups, sugar-coated pills and fruit flavors for drinks. There were only a few employees, mostly family members. J. K. Lilly, then fifteen, washed bottles and ran errands for his father.

Business began to boom thanks to the Lilly family's hard work—and the Colonel's vision. He had chosen to launch his business in Indianapolis because the city was the hub for several major railroads; the rails would be crucial for the major drug-making company that Colonel Lilly dreamed about from the beginning.

By 1879, three years after the business opened, sales of quinine (a medicine used to treat malaria and other diseases) had increased ten times. With the family business thriving, Colonel Eli Lilly turned his attention to his community. How could he help improve Indianapolis?

Colonel Lilly decided to become the key player in dozens of civic efforts. He was among twenty-five business leaders who founded a society to co-ordinate all of the charities in Indianapolis, sort of an early version of today's United Way. Colonel Lilly also initiated efforts to improve Indian-apolis' water supply and started the group that eventually became the Indianapolis Chamber of Commerce.

His emphasis on upgrading the quality of life for Hoosiers set an example for his family members, particularly a grandson also named Eli Lilly. Young Eli loved to listen to his grandfather's exciting stories about the Civil War. The Colonel crusaded to make certain that Hoosiers who fought and died in that horrible conflict would not be forgotten. His crusade led to construction of what has become the permanent symbol of Indianapolis.

In the final years of his life, Colonel Lilly devoted most of his energy to raising money for a 288-foot-tall limestone monument to the bravery of fallen Hoosier soldiers. Many of them had been the Colonel's friends and

Four generations of Lillys are shown in this family photo from 1946: (from left) Eli ("Mr. Eli"); his father, J. K. Sr.; and J. K. Jr. Seated is J. K. Lilly III, holding Eli II. (Courtesy of Eli Lilly and Company Archives)

neighbors. (About 210,000 Hoosiers fought in the Civil War; there were more than 24,000 casualties from Indiana.) In 1888, construction began on the Soldiers and Sailors Monument; it's in the center of what is now called Monument Circle—the heart of downtown Indianapolis.

The Colonel—who was a Democrat and a Republican at different stages of his life—turned down all offers to run for public office so he could focus on the monument and his other civic projects. He died of cancer at age sixty in 1898. The Soldiers and Sailors Monument was completed in 1901 and dedicated in a ceremony the next year.

The Lilly family

The young grandson who listened so intently to Colonel Eli Lilly's Civil War stories would grow up to oversee the family business' transition into a worldwide operation. Eli Lilly (1885–1977) also would become famous for his philanthropy (gift-giving). Thanks to his efforts and generosity, many aspects of life in Indiana—from schools and churches to the arts and museums—have been enormously enhanced.

The plainspoken man known as "Mr. Eli" was the son of J. K. Lilly. By the time "Mr. Eli" became president of Eli Lilly and Company in 1932, the business was making medicines that would have been completely unknown to the Colonel. In the 1920s, the company began distributing insulin, which helps control the blood sugar of people with the disease of diabetes. (In the 1980s, Eli Lilly and Company began making and selling Prozac, a medicine that relieves depression and other disorders.)

Mr. Eli is credited with applying the techniques of mass production to the drug industry—and creating thousands of jobs. Despite his enormous wealth, Mr. Eli had a blunt-speaking, "average Joe" personality. He regularly ate apple pie with his employees in the company cafeteria and, to relax, enjoyed woodworking. He was an avid historian who wrote books on the woodland Indians and served as a leader of the Indiana Historical Society.

Above all else, Eli Lilly is fondly remembered for his gift-giving. In 1937, he helped form Lilly Endowment, which has given millions of dollars to everything from Orchard Day School in Indianapolis and Wabash College in Crawfordsville to Conner Prairie Settlement, the "living history" museum in Hamilton County. (Mr. Eli was a history and art buff.) The company shifted from family control to become a public corporation by the time Mr. Eli died at the age of ninety-one.

Decades later, readers of *The Indianapolis Star* overwhelmingly named Eli Lilly as the "Greatest Hoosier of the 20th Century." They said they voted for him not because he became enormously rich or even because he created thousands of jobs. Indiana residents said Mr. Eli was the century's greatest Hoosier because of the impact he had with his gift giving. Lilly Endowment even helped pay for a baseball diamond for children in tiny Liberty, Indiana.

Fun fact: At one point, Mr. Eli told a school administrator: "You know, in running a business, you quickly understand the importance of people getting along. All of us of all ages need to know how to do that."

Carl Fisher

The man who helped begin the world-famous Indianapolis Motor Speedway had a life like a roller coaster ride. **Carl Fisher** enjoyed plenty of highs—and suffered a lot of low moments. He became enormously wealthy, but was practically poor by the time he died.

Amid all of the ups and downs:

Fisher was a stunt (trick) bicyclist, despite having weak eyes and wearing thick glasses. He thrilled—and terrified—people in downtown Indianapolis by stringing a tight-rope between the upper floors of the city's two tallest office build-ings. Then, he pedaled across on his bicycle, defying death.

He drove one of the first cars in Indiana. (And he owned a five-car garage at a time when most Hoosier families didn't even have one car.)

Fisher helped start the racetrack that brought lasting fame to Ind-ianapolis.

And he created one of the first re-sorts (vacation spots) in Florida by turning a swamp into Miami Beach.

Carl Fisher started out poor. He was born in **Greensburg** in 1874 and quit school at about age twelve to work

Carl Fisher, Speedway founder. (Indianapolis Motor Speedway)

The Indianapolis 500 draws more than a quarter of a million fans from around the world to the Indianapolis Motor Speedway. Here, popular driver Scott Sharp makes a pit stop during the race in 2000. (Stephen Baker)

as a grocery store clerk. By saving six hundred dollars, Fisher was able to open a bicycle repair shop in Indianapolis when he was just seventeen years old. He started the daredevil stunts—including the tightrope ride above downtown—to promote the bicycle shop. Business boomed.

Then came the invention of the automobile; sensing opportunities, Fisher opened an auto dealership in 1902. He created the Speedway as a testing area for cars with the help of several partners: A. C. Newby, the owner of a bicycle track; James Allison, the owner of a headlight-making company; and businessman Frank Wheeler.

In the first race at the Speedway in 1909, Fisher even was a competitor. It was a hot-air balloon race in which he piloted a balloon called "Indiana." Two years later in 1911, the Speedway was the setting for the first Indianapolis 500 auto race, which has thrilled millions of people nearly every May since then.

Soon, though, Fisher began spending most of his time in Florida. In an era long before air conditioning—when most of Florida was swampland—people thought Fisher was crazy when he built Miami Beach. He ignored them, and the seaside city became very popular with vacationers.

A hurricane hit Miami Beach in 1926, though. Although the city was rebuilt, Fisher lost huge amounts of money. That's why he nearly was penniless—and almost forgotten in Indiana—when he died in 1939.

Tony Hulman

More than twenty-five years after Carl Fisher left the running of the Indianapolis Motor Speedway to others, the famous racetrack nearly was shut down. It was rescued in the 1940s by one of Indiana's wealthiest men, Terre Haute businessman Anton J. "Tony" Hulman Jr.

He bought the Speedway in 1945 after it had been neglected during World War II. Because of the war, there were no races from 1942 through 1945—and grass even was growing in parts of the racetrack when Hulman bought it.

Hulman, who became known as "Mr. Speedway," quickly launched an improvement program. He poured millions of dollars into the Speedway, returning the track to its former glory.

He was born in 1901; his father had a successful grocery business in Terre Haute. An excellent athlete, young Tony was one of the country's top high school and college track stars and pole vaulters just before 1920.

After he took over the family business, Hulman expanded it tremendously. He became a multimillionaire and at times owned everything from a baking powder mill (where the Clabber Girl brand was made) to newspapers, radio stations, and a hotel in Terre Haute. Hulman oversaw the Speedway for more than thirty years until his death in 1977.

"Hardly a day goes by that someone doesn't come up to me and tell me about some terrific things that he did," says Tony George, his grandson. George (who was born in 1959) has been president of the Speedway since 1989.

In August 1994, with NASCAR's Brickyard 400, George introduced stock car racing to the Speedway's oval-shaped track. It has since become an annual event.

In September 2000, the track was the site of its first Formula One race, a type of auto racing enjoyed by millions of Europeans, including royalty.

Formula One cars are open-wheeled like Indy 500 race cars. But the Formula One cars race clockwise at the Speedway, which is the reverse of the direction for the 500-Mile Race and the Brickyard 400. Also, for the Formula One race, the course is altered to feature thirteen turns zigzagging across the Speedway infield. Called the U.S. Grand Prix, it is the only Formula One race staged in the United States.

Michael Graves

The Indianapolis Art Center. The headquarters of Thomson Consumer Electronics. The $35 million NCAA Headquarters and Hall of Champions.

Those impressive buildings in **Indianapolis** have been designed by an architect famous around the world—and he grew up not far from his creations.

Michael Graves (who was born in Indianapolis in 1934) designed the Indianapolis Art Center in the Broad Ripple neighborhood; he had graduated from nearby Broad Ripple High School in 1952. The art center is a marvel of the imagination with its pastel panels and unusual design. Viewed from overhead, it almost looks like the stick figure of a human being.

Graves' connection to the art center goes beyond just being the architect who designed the building. The center has exhibited many of Graves' smaller creations: clocks, patio furniture, toasters, and whistling teakettles. The famous architect designs all of those products as well as buildings.

In his hometown, Graves also designed the NCAA Headquarters and Hall of Champions, which opened in the fall of 1999 in White River State Park. He designed the Hall of Champions to look like a sports stadium, with sports banners flying from flagpoles on the top.

Michael Graves, architect and designer. (Bill Phelps)

The Indianapolis Art Center in Broad Ripple opened in 1986. (Courtesy of Indianapolis Art Center)

Graves' designs perk up functional household items, such as this whistling teakettle and egg-shaped toaster. (Photos courtesy of Michael Graves & Associates)

Around the country, Graves has been the architect of more than two hundred buildings, including libraries, museums, and Disney corporate offices in Burbank, California.

Known for his dramatic use of color and geometric forms (the toaster he designed is shaped like an egg), Graves is considered a pioneer of a type of architecture known as "post-modernist."

After graduating from Broad Ripple High, Graves studied architecture at the University of Cincinnati and Harvard University. For most of his career, he has lived in Princeton, New Jersey; he is a professor of architecture at Princeton University.

His home in Princeton—an architectural wonder known as "The Warehouse"—is itself a national tourist attraction, with its lush gardens, wisteria vines and tiled bricks.

In 1999, President Clinton awarded Graves the National Medal of Arts.

Hoosier astronauts

Why have so many astronauts lived in Indiana? A major reason involves Purdue University in **West Lafayette**. The university is nicknamed the "Mother of Astronauts" because so many of them have attended Purdue from the very beginning of the American space program in the 1950s.

Starting with Virgil "Gus" Grissom, one of the original group of astronauts selected by the National Aeronautics and Space Administration (NASA); continuing through Neil Armstrong, the first man to walk on the moon in 1969 (he was a 1955 Purdue graduate); to doctor-scientist David Wolf, who lived on the Mir space station in 1997–1998—there has been a Purdue link to almost every NASA mission.

In addition, more Midwesterners have been chosen as astronauts than natives of any other region of the country.

"This may sound corny," says astronaut Greg Harbaugh (a member of Purdue's class of '78), "but I think NASA craves good, solid Midwesterners, wholesome types raised with the work ethic."

Following is a look at some space explorers with especially deep Hoosier roots.

Virgil "Gus" Grissom

As one of the original seven American astronauts chosen in 1959, **Virgil "Gus" Grissom** of **Mitchell**, Indiana, was a true pioneer.

He had several claims to fame. In 1961, Grissom became the second American to go up in space. (Only Alan Shepard of New Hampshire went up sooner.) Four years later, Gus Grissom orbited the Earth in a Gemini spacecraft. That made him the first person to travel in space twice. Sadly, his career was cut short when he was killed in a tragic accident during a NASA ground test.

Born in 1926, Grissom showed promise early on in Mitchell, which is a small city in southern Indiana. He excelled in the Boy Scouts, graduated from Purdue and was an Air Force officer and fighter pilot during the Korean War in the early 1950s. (**Fun fact:** Grissom nearly was rejected from the history-making group of original astronauts because he suffered from hay fever. According to legend, he saved himself with this classic line: "There won't be any ragweed pollen in space.")

Although his fellow astronauts loved Grissom, he became a controversial figure to some people because of the way his first space flight ended in 1961. When his Mercury capsule splashed down in the Atlantic Ocean, some people suspected Grissom panicked. They said his frantic efforts to escape the capsule caused it to sink to the bottom of the ocean, loaded with scientific data. (Rescuers from a helicopter picked up Gus.) Recent research indicates, though, that the capsule's hatch could have suddenly blown open—just as Grissom always insisted.

In any case, he is remembered as an all-American hero by most Hoosiers. And people across the world were saddened on January 27, 1967, when Grissom was killed at age forty. He was serving as commander of the Apollo One spacecraft during what was supposed to be a routine ground test at Cape Kennedy in Florida. During the countdown, a fire engulfed the Apollo. Grissom and two other astronauts were killed instantly.

An Air Force base in north central Indiana was renamed in Grissom's honor. In 1999, readers of *The Indianapolis Star* chose Gus Grissom as one of the "Ten Greatest Hoosiers of the 20th Century."

David Wolf

He is the first native of **Indianapolis** to go up in space. **David Wolf**, who is a physician, scientist and engineer as well as an astronaut, was one of seven Columbia crew members who spent fourteen days (then a NASA record) in space in 1993.

Four years later, Wolf was in outer space much longer—and drew world-wide attention. He spent 119 days—from September of 1997 to January of 1998—living and working in the Russian space station Mir.

David Wolf (who was born in 1956), a graduate of North Central High School and the Indiana University School of Medicine as well as Purdue, took several Hoosier souvenirs with him to Mir, which orbited the Earth from 250 miles up. During his stay on Mir, David also performed scientific and medical experiments; he sent e-mail from outer space to students at several Indiana schools. He also took a spacewalk from Mir, stepping out in his spacesuit to a temperature of minus-150 degrees Fahrenheit.

Ever since his boyhood, Wolf day-dreamed about going up in space. He grew up to become more than an astronaut. As a doctor, he has worked as a flight surgeon. He's an electrical engineer and a pilot. As a scientist, he headed a team that developed a device used in cancer research. An adventure seeker, Wolf has explored the Arctic Circle (around the North Pole) and, as a

Virgil "Gus" Grissom, a space pioneer as one of the original American astronauts. (Indiana Historical Society)

Astronaut David Wolf in his space-walking suit. (NASA photo courtesy of Dottie Wolf)

Astronaut Jerry Ross receives a civic award from gospel singer Sandi Patty—another legendary Hoosier. (Courtesy of *The Indianapolis Star*)

doctor, he traveled to remote parts of the Amazon River in South America to deliver medical care to natives.

Since coming down from Mir, he has appeared on CNN and other TV networks as a space analyst.

"I've gone from being thrilled by adventure to loving the technology to the point I'm at now, being most interested in research benefits (in space) for Earth," Wolf says.

Mir plunged to Earth and burned up in March of 2000. But at the Johnson Space Center in Houston, Texas, David Wolf is helping design and build a new space center. Sixteen countries are involved in the project, which is to be called the International Space Station.

Jerry Ross

Known for his great sense of humor, Jerry Ross of Crown Point, Indiana, entertained a TV audience of millions by somersaulting in space in 1991.

When the astronaut was told to come back to the space shuttle Atlantis after his somersault, he grumbled: "Rats." (TV commentators then compared him to "a boy who hears his mother call for dinner.")

On a serious note, Ross holds an impressive record. The Hoosier has spent more hours "spacewalking" than any person in history. And on six flights aboard the space shuttle, he has logged twenty million miles.

Ross, who was born in 1948, grew up in a rural area near Crown Point and made scrapbooks about outer space as a boy. But he says he never imagined that he would walk on a mechanical arm in space, as Ross did during a mission in 1985.

During his 1996 spacewalk—which included the somersaults—he fixed an antenna stuck against the side of a $167 million space laboratory.

Jerry Ross has become a popular public speaker across the country. He jokes that he enjoyed "home cooking" in space because his wife—Karen Pearson Ross, a native of Sheridan, Indiana—supervises the packaging of astronauts' dehydrated food. She, too, is a Purdue graduate.

Other Hoosier astronauts

- Donald Williams, a farm boy from tiny Otterbein, Indiana, grew up to become commander of the crew on the space shuttle Atlantis in 1989. Williams, who was born in 1942, served as a cadet on a Navy submarine and as a test pilot before becoming an astronaut. Of traveling in outer space, he says, "The view is awesome."

- Crawfordsville native Joe Allen (born in 1937) graduated from DePauw University and became an astronaut-scientist. He was aboard two space shuttle flights in the 1980s. From the shuttle Discovery in 1984, Joe Allen helped rescue two stranded communication satellites for return to Earth in the first space salvage mission.

- Other astronauts include Mark N. Brown (born in 1951), a native of Valparaiso, and Janice Voss, who was born in South Bend in 1956. Both of them are graduates of Purdue, "Mother of Astronauts."

Hoosier Entrepreneurs

The Wright Brothers

History was made on December 17, 1903, when two brothers, **Wilbur and Orville Wright**, designed and flew an airplane they made. Their plane was in the air only twelve seconds, but it was the first time a motor-driven machine carried a human being in flight.

The "twelve seconds that changed the world" occurred near Kitty Hawk, North Carolina, hundreds of miles from Indiana. But the Wright brothers had Hoosier roots. Their father, the Reverend Milton Wright, was a bishop in the United Brethren Church; he was born in Rush County, Indiana, in 1828.

Reverend Wright and his wife, Susan, had five children. The family traveled frequently as Reverend Wright preached at various churches in Ohio and Indiana. Wilbur, the third son, was born in 1867 near the small town of **Millville** in eastern Indiana. Then the Wrights moved again, and Orville was born in Dayton, Ohio, in 1871. For a time, the Wright family also lived in Fairmount, Indiana, the small town that later would be the boyhood home of movie star James Dean and *Garfield* cartoonist Jim Davis.

Wilbur and Orville Wright had very different personalities. Wilbur was an honor student and considered going to Yale University; Orville enjoyed playing

On May 30, 1910, the Wright brothers visited the Indianapolis Motor Speedway, where this photo was taken. Wilbur (third from the right) and Orville (second from the right) were planning an air show that they sponsored at the Speedway in June 1910. (Wright State University)

"hooky" and eventually dropped out of school. Even so, the brothers made a great team. When bicycles became popular across America in the 1890s, they opened a bicycle shop in Dayton.

Soon the country was buzzing with talk about the possibility of "flying machines"; some experts predicted that bicycle makers would be the ones to make the first successful airplane. After all, didn't bicycle makers have to deal with steady balance and light-weight material?

In 1896, Orville came down with typhoid fever. Wilbur spent days at his brother's bedside, where he began reading about gliders and flying machines. The brothers decided they would become airplane pioneers. They contacted the U.S. Weather Service for suggestions about the best place to test their gliders. The brothers settled on Kitty Hawk, North Carolina, because of its sand dunes that would cushion landings and its steady winds. Their famous twelve-second flight occurred over an area near Kitty Hawk with a scary name: Kill Devil Hill.

It was Orville who was in the only pilot's seat. (Actually, there wasn't even *one* seat: Orville had to lie down on the plane during the flight.) Orville was chosen because he had won a coin toss.

Their first airplane had wings forty feet long; when a pilot was aboard, it weighed seven hundred and fifty pounds. The Wright brothers designed and built the plane's gasoline engine themselves. All in all, their plane cost less than a thousand dollars to build.

For the rest of their lives, the brothers spent most of their time in Dayton. That's where Wilbur Wright died in 1912, and Orville in 1948.

But their Indiana roots haven't been forgotten. There is a Wilbur Wright memorial birthplace near Millville, Indiana. It's open to the public for tours.

The Wright brothers with one of their early aircraft in 1904. The brothers were testing the propellers on their aircraft, a Flyer III, at Simms Station in Dayton, Ohio. The Flyer III was a slightly altered version of their Flyer, the aircraft used in the first flight at Kitty Hawk, North Carolina. (Wright State University)

Orville Redenbacher

The man known as "The Popcorn King" was a Hoosier through and through. Orville Redenbacher (1907–1995) was an Indiana farm boy who grew up to create the best-selling popcorn in America. He is credited with greatly increasing popcorn's popularity—or "pop"-ularity—across the country by creating a type that was much fluffier and whiter. His popcorn also was able to expand forty times its original size when popped.

A grandfatherly man who almost always wore a bow tie, Redenbacher became famous by putting his photo on the label of his popcorn and by appearing in dozens of TV commercials.

Redenbacher grew up on his family's farm near Brazil, Indiana. As a student at Brazil High School, he won state championships in 4-H club contests. Young Orville attended Purdue University; he paid his way by scrubbing hog houses and tending chickens.

He became a farm agent in Vigo County. For more than forty years, Redenbacher experimented with three thousand types of popcorn before he

Orville Redenbacher called himself "just a funny-looking farmer with a funny-sounding name." But he became king of the popcorn industry. Experts say he made the first major changes in popcorn since the Indians introduced it to the Pilgrims in the 1600s. (Photofest)

hit the jackpot. In 1976, Orville Redenbacher Original Gourmet Popcorn became the top-selling popcorn in the United States. It is still Number One.

For many years, Redenbacher lived in **Valparaiso**, which continues to hold an annual popcorn parade and festival in his honor.

Fun Fact: The beloved "Popcorn King" always ate his popcorn with salt, but no butter.

A recipe with popcorn

PEANUT BUTTER AND JELLY THUMBPRINT NO-BAKE POPCORN COOKIES
(Yield: 18 cookies)

UTENSILS:
Large bowl, medium saucepan, and a spoon

INGREDIENTS:
2 quarts Orville's popped popcorn (make sure that there are no hard, unpopped kernels of corn)
1 cup light corn syrup
1 cup creamy peanut butter
6 tablespoons fruit jam (strawberry, apricot, raspberry, etc.)*

DIRECTIONS:
1. Put popcorn in a large bowl.
2. In a saucepan, over medium-high heat, bring the corn syrup to a boil, and boil for three minutes.
3. Stir in the peanut butter.
4. Working quickly, pour the peanut butter mixture over the popcorn, tossing gently to coat.
5. Allow to cool for ten minutes.
6. Roll the popcorn mixture into eighteen two-inch balls.
7. Press a thumb firmly into the center of each ball.
8. Fill each cookie center with half a teaspoon of jam.
9. Store cookies in an airtight container.

* Substitute chocolate kisses—or almost anything else that suits your fancy—for jam in the center of each cookie.

NUTRITIONAL INFORMATION: 156 calories per cookie, 0 milligrams cholesterol, 8 grams fat, 104 milligrams sodium.

Recipe adapted by Wanda Willis from *Orville Redenbacher, Popcorn King* (Summit Publishing Group, 1996) by Len Sherman.

Bill Blass and Norman Norell

On labels of stylish clothes worn by men and women around the world, you will see the name of a native Hoosier: **Bill Blass.**

For fifty years, he has been one of the world's top fashion designers. Bill Blass specializes in designing elegant evening gowns and daytime suits for women, and also sportswear for women and men.

Blass was born in **Fort Wayne** in 1922. At the age of eighteen in 1940, he left Indiana to study design in New York City, the nation's fashion capital.

"There's one thing they taught in that part of the country—manners," Blass told *The Indianapolis Star* in 1997, referring to Indiana. "The Middle West has a quality that's appealing, an ethical quality—dedication, honesty, fairness, decency."

In New York, his clients have included dozens of celebrities such as former first lady Nancy Reagan, singer-actress Barbra Streisand, and TV news-woman Barbara Walters. As a designer, Blass has been known for avoiding "extremes" in fashion; his clothes almost always have a classic look that stays in style for many years.

Blass won the fashion industry's Coty Award three times (in 1961, 1963, and 1970) and has been inducted into

Still-popular fashion designer Bill Blass at work in his studio in 1961. (Photofest)

the Fashion Hall of Fame. In 1999, Blass retired as a designer. His final runway show in New York drew tears from many fans.

Ironically, after Blass left Indiana to go to New York, he ended up with a fellow Hoosier as his mentor (teacher/role model). **Norman Norell,** a top fashion designer of the 1940s through the '60s, was one of the first Americans to become as respected as designers from France and Italy. In the early 1900s and before, Europeans set all the fashion trends. Norell helped to move Americans to the forefront.

Born Norman David Levinson in **Noblesville** in 1900, Norell changed his name as a young man, explaining "Norell" this way: "NOR for Norman, L

for Levinson. Another L for looks.") As a boy, he worked in his father's hat shop in Indianapolis.

Norell-designed dresses eventually became the most expensive in America. He died in 1972.

By that point, a third Hoosier fashion designer had become famous. He was known by a single name: **Halston.** At his birth in 1932, he had been named Roy Halston Fenwick. He grew up in **Evansville,** attended Indiana University and got his start by designing hats in New York.

Halston first made news by creating a "pillbox" hat for first lady Jacqueline Kennedy in 1961. During the 1970s, he probably was the best-known designer in the world. Halston died in 1990.

Nancy Noël

One of the country's most famous painters of children, angels, the Amish, and African wildlife lives on a rolling, forty-five-acre farm near Zionsville.

As Nancy Noël paints in her studio on the upper floor of a horse barn, she can gaze out of windows at her pet llamas (she owns twenty-five of the gentle animals), dogs, geese, and lambs.

Noël has achieved stunning business and artistic success. She owns a gallery in Indianapolis from which her artwork is shipped around the world. Top political leaders, movie stars, and other celebrities are among her clients. But she dealt with many rejections early in her life and career.

Nancy Noël began as an artist by drawing pastel portraits of children for ten dollars apiece. She thought one of her paintings—of an antique rocking horse—would make a wonderful poster. In 1982, the country's largest poster distributors told her the poster never would sell; twelve companies in New York rejected her.

So Noël returned to Indiana, published the *Antique Rocking Horse* poster herself, and it became a hit. Now, she has a two-year waiting list of wealthy clients who want her to paint portraits of their children. Rather than ten

Artist Nancy Noël, with her pet cockatoo and cat and surrounded by some of her paintings, in her farmhouse studio in Zionsville. (Courtesy of Noël Studio)

dollars, they pay at least five thousand dollars per painting.

By the time she had painted *Antique Rocking Horse*, Noël (who was born in Indianapolis in 1945) was used to struggling. As a girl in Catholic schools in Indianapolis, she had difficulty learning. (Years later, Noël learned why: At age forty-four, she was diagnosed with dyslexia, a learning disorder.) Fortunately, a Catholic nun, one of her teachers, encouraged Noël to pursue her passion: creating art.

"Nancy always has been a sensitive person," says Sister Alice Louise Potts, her former teacher—who remains today one of Noël's closest friends.

With her artwork, Noël uses a variety of media, including watercolors, oils, acrylics, pencils, markers, and pastels. Celebrities who own her oil paintings include movie stars Robert Redford and Jane Seymour, the Beach Boys (popular singers from the 1960s), and former South African president Nelson Mandela.

Noël became fascinated with Africa in the 1980s. Since then, she has traveled there more than a dozen times—sometimes to paint African wildlife and tribal people, and sometimes to help with causes such as saving the rhinoceros from hunters and funding orphanages and schools. (A preschool at an orphanage in the country of Kenya is even named in her honor.)

In Indiana, she has long been popular for her paintings of the Amish, spiritual people who lead simple lives without electricity and cars. She also has illustrated five books of angel poetry and images. They include *On Earth As It Is In Heaven* (1999), the story of a child angel named Rosie, and *I Am Wherever You Are* (2000).

"From now on," Noël says, "my primary concentration as an artist will be on deeply spiritual themes."

Jim Davis

When he was a boy growing up on his family's cattle farm near Fairmount, Jim Davis was frequently sick and confined to bed.

The future world-famous cartoonist and creator of Garfield suffered from severe asthma, a breathing disorder. Years later, Jim, who was born in 1945, learned that his asthma probably was aggravated by the hay, straw, pollen and other farm substances that were in the air around his home.

He was stuck in bed for months at a stretch—but instead of feeling sorry for himself and wallowing in his misery, Jim started to doodle.

"The only way I could get out of the house was in my imagination," he explains.

Thanks to his constant drawing and doodling, Jim kept improving as an artist. He also found inspiration for his future creation of cantankerous, mischievous Garfield: Twenty-five cats lived on his family's farm.

When Jim grew older, he attended the same high school as another famous Hoosier, movie actor James Dean. About fifteen years after Dean graduated from Fairmount High School, Jim Davis showed up—and had the same mentor—Adeline Nall, a drama

Sometimes Garfield seems to be everywhere, doesn't he? Here, the world's most famous cartoon cat surrounds his Hoosier creator, Jim Davis. (GARFIELD @ Paws Inc. All rights reserved.)

and speech coach at Fairmount High.

"I was painfully shy, and she pulled me out of it," Davis recalls. "I have no idea what she saw in me, but she cast me in four plays."

Davis eventually conquered both asthma and shyness. After studying art at Ball State University, he created the world's most famous cartoon cat—and the Indiana farm boy became a millionaire.

The *Garfield* comic strip, which began in 1978, is carried in twenty-five hundred newspapers, from Muncie (the city closest to PAWS Inc., Davis' business headquarters) to Tokyo, Japan, and New Delhi, India. Products featuring the lazy orange cat (a typical Garfield quip: "I'd like mornings better if they started later.") range from underwear, posters and greeting cards to the stuffed dolls with suction cup paws seen in thousands of car windows.

More than 220 million people read the comic strip every day.

A nature lover, Jim Davis continues to live in Delaware County near PAWS Inc., which is on a thirty-acre, wooded retreat.

Did you know?

- Garfield wasn't Jim Davis's first comic strip. His first attempt failed. A cartoon featuring a gnat named Gnorm, it appeared in only one newspaper, the *Pendleton* (Indiana) *Times*. Jim ended the strip by having a giant shoe crush the gnat.

- Jim Davis and Garfield share a favorite food: lasagna. Only after he received letters from dozens of pet owners did Jim realize that many cats truly *do* love lasagna and other Italian cuisine. "I'm told it's the tomato sauce that really appeals to them," he says.

- Garfield has starred in thirteen TV specials and forty books since the first book, *Garfield at Large*, was published in 1980. In 1983, seven Garfield books appeared simultaneously on *The New York Times* bestseller list.

Legends in the Arts

Lew Wallace

He was a general in the Civil War for the Union Army. **Lew Wallace** also was a diplomat to Turkey. And in the late 1870s, he served as governor of the new territory of New Mexico, where he dealt with notorious gunslingers, including Billy the Kid.

None of that, though, is the main reason that glory-seeking Wallace (1827–1905) of **Crawfordsville** remains famous a century after his death.

He wrote an epic novel that was read by more people in its time than any other book except the Bible. *Ben-Hur: A Tale of the Christ* (1880) is a historical romance about Christians in the early days of the Roman Empire and the coming of Christ. The main character is a proud, handsome Jewish prince—and former slave—named Judah Ben-Hur. He seeks revenge against Messala, his former best friend who turns into a bitter enemy. The book includes chariot races, pirates, camels, gladiators, and a look at people suffering from the horrible disease of leprosy—as well as appearances by such biblical figures as the Three Wise Men.

When Wallace wrote *Ben-Hur*, he had never visited the Holy Land or

Lew Wallace was a soldier, diplomat, lawyer and politician. He's best remembered, though, as the author of *Ben-Hur* (1880). (Indiana Historical Society)

Rome, the main settings of the novel.

Even so, the book won thousands of fans, including church-goers and non-believers, Catholics, and Protestants—even U.S. President James Garfield. (In April 1881, Garfield stayed up until the wee hours several nights at the White House because he could not put *Ben-Hur* down. Later that year, President Garfield appointed Wallace as America's minister to Turkey.)

The author of *Ben-Hur* was born in Brookville, a bustling village in southeastern Indiana. Lew Wallace followed a boyhood dream of becoming a soldier, starting at age nineteen in the Mexican War in 1846.

Aside from *Ben-Hur*, his major fame came as a military leader during the Civil War. Fighting for the Union Army, Wallace helped capture Fort Donelson in Tennessee from the Confederates (South). Some Hoosiers consider General Wallace to have been the state's most distinguished Civil War veteran. Other historians, however, are critical of how he commanded his forces in battles late in the war.

In any case, Lew Wallace chose to spend the last years of his life in Crawfordsville with his wife, Susan. They lived in a home with a large author's studio filled with books. It has been declared a National Historic Landmark and is open for tours.

Fun facts

- Lew Wallace was the son of Indiana's sixth governor. His father, David Wallace, was governor in the late 1830s. (Wallace's mother, Esther, died when he was just seven years old in 1834.)

- Young Wallace was a thrill-seeker even as a boy. He had a bad habit of skipping school to play in the Wabash River near his boyhood home in Covington.

- After the Civil War, Wallace helped preside over a famous trial. He was a member of the military court that tried the people who had conspired to help John Wilkes Booth assassinate President Abraham Lincoln.

- The movie version of *Ben-Hur* (1959) won eleven Academy Awards, then a record. The blockbuster stars Charlton Heston as Ben-Hur and features a thrilling chariot race.

- Lew Wallace served on the commission to build the Soldiers and Sailors Monument on Monument Circle in downtown Indianapolis to honor Civil War veterans. He resigned in 1895, though, when the commission decided to put a statue of "Miss Victory" atop the monument. "The Civil War was fought by men, and no woman ought to be on top of the monument," he said. What do you think?

Gene Stratton-Porter

Can you imagine plunging into a swamp full of mud, scum and critters like muskrats, mosquitoes, gnats and—worst of all—poisonous snakes?

Well, dangerous marshlands like that were exactly where Gene Stratton-Porter spent hours and hours by herself. Stratton-Porter (1863–1924) loved wildlife, particularly birds, and wanted to alert the rest of America to the natural wonders of the swamps near her homes in northern Indiana.

So even though Stratton-Porter's neighbors thought she was weird—in her day, middle-class housewives just did not traipse through swamps—she regularly pulled on hip boots and plunged into snake-infested muck. Stratton-Porter often carried a bulky camera that her eight-year-old daughter gave her as a Christmas gift. With her books and close-up pictures of birds and other wildlife in Indiana marshlands, Stratton-Porter became a famous novelist and photographer.

Shortly before her fortieth birthday in 1903, Stratton-Porter had her first book published. *The Song of the Cardinal* was inspired when Stratton-Porter discovered the body of a bright red cardinal. It had been shot in target practice near Limberlost Swamp, a vast, unexplored marshland one mile

Novelist and early environmentalist Gene Stratton-Porter as she looked about 1920. (Indiana State Museum and Historic Sites)

Stratton-Porter was famous for photos of birds such as this one, taken around 1910. (Indiana State Museum and Historic Sites)

away from the home that she loved. It was in the town of **Geneva**. The plot of Stratton-Porter's novel is about a lovesick redbird that is stalked by a hunter near Limberlost Swamp.

The swamp also became the setting for Stratton-Porter's next book, *Freckles* (1904), one of her most famous novels and a national best seller. Her other best sellers included *A Girl of the Limberlost* (1909) and *Laddie* (1913).

Having grown up on a farm in Wabash County, Stratton-Porter was fascinated by nature all of her life. Her father, a part-time preacher, taught her that animals and plants were God's gifts and, as such, deserved respect. According to Stratton-Porter's daughter, Jeannette Porter Meehan, Gene often nursed wounded birds in the family's house. She even kept boxes of baby caterpillars indoors and allowed young moths and butterflies to flutter around.

Her family lived in two homes that came to be known as the Limberlost Cabins. The first cabin was their home in Geneva. Stratton-Porter built the second Limberlost Cabin on one hundred and twenty acres that she bought near **Sylvan Lake**, also in northern Indiana. She planted three thousand flowers, trees, shrubs and vines at the second Limberlost estate, which she called Wildflower Woods.

Angered at the destruction of nature by lumbermen and farmers, Stratton-Porter became an environmentalist—although the term hadn't even been invented in the 1910s. As part of her crusade to save swamps and woodlands, she clashed with Indiana politicians and worked to change state laws.

Near the end of her life, Stratton-Porter moved to southern California. Some of her books were being turned into movies, so she formed a film-production company. She was killed in an automobile accident in 1924.

The plot of *A Girl of the Limberlost*

Elnora Comstock is a poor, lonely girl who lives on a farm in Adams County in northeastern Indiana.

Life is tough for Elnora. Her father has died. Her mother, Kate, is overworked and bitter. And Elnora dreams of getting an education, but doesn't know how to pay for it. Fortunately, young Elnora finds a perfect place to escape her sorrows: the mysterious Limberlost swamp near her farm. The swamp's moths and butterflies fascinate Elnora. She even finds a way to use her love of nature to pay for her schooling. At school, Elnora is introduced to the world of music—and she falls in love with it.

Elnora is the heroine of *A Girl of the Limberlost*, a novel by Gene Stratton-Porter. The book has been read by millions of girls and boys since it was written nearly one hundred years ago in 1909. Still popular with children, *A Girl of the Limberlost* was made into a TV movie in 1990.

An excerpt from *Freckles*

In *Freckles*, Gene Stratton-Porter's first best seller, the main character, Freckles, is an orphan with one leg; he explores the Limberlost Swamp, which is the home of wildlife ranging from owls to rattlesnakes. Stratton-Porter described Freckles' experience in the swamp this way:

A prowling wildcat missed its catch and screamed with rage. A lost fox bayed incessantly for its mate. The hair on the back of Freckles' neck rose like bristles, and his knees wavered under him. He could not see if the dreaded snakes were on the trail, nor, in the pandemonium, hear the rattle for which McLean had cautioned him to listen. He stood rooted to the ground in an agony of fear.

T. C. Steele

The best-known painter from Indiana didn't only make himself famous. T. C. Steele also made Brown County, Indiana, famous because he captured the spectacular beauty of its hills, woods, trees and flowers in his landscape paintings.

Believe it or not, most friends of Theodore Clement Steele (1847–1926) thought he was a bit crazy when he announced in 1907 that he had bought wooded land in Brown County. He was sixty years old by then. T. C. Steele had become a member of high society—the elite—in Indianapolis. He painted the portraits of wealthy or famous Hoosiers; they included several of the legendary men and women profiled in this book such as **Benjamin Harrison** and **May Wright Sewall**. As a popular artist, Steele lived in a ritzy house in Indianapolis with lush gardens and vines. He had a beard, which was very stylish then.

Why would such a successful painter want to live in "the sticks" of rural Brown County? In 1907, when Steele built his house there, hilly Brown County was isolated from the rest of the state. There were only a few dirt roads—and they were rugged, steep and muddy. (It took an entire day to get to **Bloomington**, the nearest town of

Legendary artist T. C. Steele as painted by fellow Hoosier artist Wayman Adams. (From the collection of the Indiana State Museum and Historic Sites)

T. C. Steele's *The Haystacks*, painted about 1910, depicts a Brown County scene. (From the collection of the Indiana State Museum and Historic Sites)

any size.) Most residents of Brown County had so little schooling that they did not know how to read or write. They barely managed to make a living by growing their own food.

Many of Steele's friends feared that the painter wasn't thinking clearly when he bought the Brown County land. They knew he was still deeply saddened over the death of his wife, Libbie, who had passed away eight years earlier.

Steele had a second surprise for his friends: About the time that he bought the land in Brown County, he married again. His second wife, Selma, got her first look at what was to be her new home—the Brown County house—on their wedding day in August 1907.

Soon it all began to make sense. From his Brown County home—which T. C. Steele called "The House of the Singing Winds"—he produced stunning artwork: paintings of the scenery. He loved the views of Brown County. From his hilltop porch, he could see for twenty miles. Near The House of the Singing Winds, Selma planted beautiful flower gardens. When the flowers bloomed, Steele set up his canvases and painted them; he sold the artwork for high prices.

The Steeles became friendly with their Brown County neighbors—who at first were suspicious of the "city artist"—by inviting them to The House of the Singing Winds to hear music. (The Steeles owned a piano, one of the few in the entire county.) The Steeles hired workers to bring their drinking water from a well in **Belmont**, a small town nearby.

Eventually, Steele built his "dream" studio next to his Brown County home; the studio looks like a huge barn.

When roads to Bloomington improved, Steele frequently traveled to Indiana University. He became an "artist-in-residence" there. As IU students strolled around campus, they would see him with his easel, canvas, and paintbrushes.

Steele always had enjoyed young people. Born in the small town of **Gosport**, Indiana, he had grown up in another small town, **Waveland**. He taught drawing there when he was only thirteen years old. (Later, he studied at a well-known art school in Germany.)

Because he started so young—and kept so busy—Steele produced about fifteen hundred paintings over his lifetime.

Once the famous artist painted Brown County scenes, people started to flock there to look at the area's natural beauty.

The Hoosier Group

T. C. Steele was the most famous member of a group of talented Indiana painters in the late 1800s and early 1900s. The five painters came to be known as the Hoosier Group after they were praised at an art exhibit in Chicago in 1894. Art critics felt the Indiana painters captured the beauty of Indiana in a fresh way.

In addition to Steele, members of the Hoosier Group included

- J. Ottis Adams (1851–1927), who loved to paint scenes of the Whitewater River near Brookville, Indiana. For a few years, Adams and Steele had side-by-side studios in a home in Brookville called The Hermitage.

- William Forsyth (1854–1935), who frequently painted the scenery near his home in the Indianapolis neighborhood of Irvington. In particular, he created paintings of Pleasant Run Creek. (Like Steele, Adams and Forsyth traveled to Germany to study painting at a well-known art school there.)

- Richard B. Gruelle (1851–1914), who lived near his friend, poet James Whitcomb Riley, in the Lockerbie neighborhood of Indianapolis. A water lover, Richard B. Gruelle often painted landscapes of the canals in the Indianapolis area. He was an entirely "self-taught" artist—that is, Gruelle taught himself to paint.

- Otto Stark (1859–1926), a much-loved teacher at the Herron School of Art in Indianapolis. Stark enjoyed painting outdoor scenes. But he also frequently used local children as models for his artwork.

T. C. Steele died in his beloved House of the Singing Winds in 1926. The house and barn-like studio are open to the public as part of the T. C. Steele State Historic Site. They are fascinating to tour, in part because Selma saved almost everything that belonged to her husband—even his cigar and its ashes.

Above the fireplace in The House of the Singing Winds, Steele had this motto inscribed:

"Every morning I take off my hat to the Beauty of the World."

Johnny Gruelle and Raggedy Ann

The world's most famous rag doll is probably a Hoosier.

Floppy, red-haired Raggedy Ann and her brother, Raggedy Andy, were created by a Hoosier, a talented cartoonist and storyteller named Johnny Gruelle.

In a way, Raggedy Ann and Raggedy Andy are the "grandchildren" of an artist in the Hoosier Group: Johnny Gruelle's father was the landscape painter Richard B. Gruelle.

The Gruelle family lived in the Lockerbie neighborhood of Indianapolis, where their neighbor was famous poet James Whitcomb Riley. Years later, Johnny Gruelle (1880–1938) based Raggedy Ann in part on a character in one of his favorite Riley poems: "Little Orphant Annie."

Before he created Raggedy Ann, Johnny Gruelle worked as a cartoonist for *The Indianapolis Star* newspaper, beginning in 1903. He became so popular that he was hired away by newspapers on the East Coast. While living there, Johnny and his wife were horrified when their thirteen-year-old daughter, Marcella, fell seriously ill.

The Raggedy Ann adventures began as bedtime stories that Johnny Gruelle told to cheer up or distract Marcella. (Sadly, she died in 1915.) He based the adventures on a floppy rag doll with shoe-button eyes owned by the Gruelle family, weaving in names and character traits from the Riley poem.

The first Raggedy Ann products sold to the American people were adventure books by Johnny Gruelle. The first book, *Raggedy Ann Stories*, was published in 1918; *Raggedy Andy Stories* came out in 1920. The floppy dolls were really spin-off products; they were created to help promote the books. In the beginning, the dolls were hand-made by members of the Gruelle family.

The Raggedy Ann and Raggedy Andy dolls were huge hits right from the start. The dolls had hair of brown yarn for the first thirty or so years, but have had red-yarn hair ever since. Johnny Gruelle wrote and illustrated one Raggedy Ann and Andy book every year until he died.

For a look at Raggedy Ann, see the painting on the floor next to artist Nancy Noël in the "Hoosier Entrepreneurs" section of this book.

Fun fact: Many of the first Raggedy Ann dolls were made with a heart sewn into their chests. The cardboard or candy hearts could easily be felt when Raggedy Ann was hugged.

James Whitcomb Riley

One of the best-known children's poets in history—and the most popular poet of his day in America—was James Whitcomb Riley. Millions of people have known this legendary man as "The Hoosier Poet," the beloved creator of such classics as "Little Orphant Annie," "When the Frost Is On the Punkin," and "The Raggedy Man."

James Whitcomb Riley (1849–1916) became an international celebrity not only because of the way he wrote, but because he was very popular as a touring entertainer. In the late 1800s and early 1900s, James Whitcomb Riley drew passionate fans—almost the way rock stars would a century later.

During Riley's performances, audiences would choke back tears, howl with glee, stomp their feet—in other words, they would be pulled through a range of emotions. Thousands of people who never got to attend one of his performances framed his poems and hung them in their parlors and kitchens.

What did this poet from Greenfield, Indiana, write about to cause such devotion?

Swimmin' holes, jack-o'-lanterns, bullfrogs, bonnets, and the simple pleasures of childhood—those are the topics of Riley poems. Consider one of his most famous poems, "When the Frost Is On the Punkin." Generations of Hoosier children have memorized the poem that begins:

> When the frost is on the punkin and
> the fodder's in the shock,
> And you hear the kyouck and gobble of
> the struttin' turkey-cock,
> And the clackin' of the guineys, and
> the cluckin' of the hens,
> And the rooster's hallylooer as he
> tiptoes on the fence;
> O, it's then's the times a feller is a-
> feelin' at his best,
> With the risin' sun to greet him from a
> night of peaceful rest.
> As he leaves the house, bareheaded,
> and goes out to feed the stock,
> When the frost is on the punkin' and
> the fodder's in the shock.

Doesn't it create an image of October in Indiana, especially out in the country? October was the month when James Whitcomb Riley was born—specifically, on October 7, 1849. The young boy known as "Jim" was named after James Whitcomb, one of Indiana's first governors. Young Jim Riley's father, Reuben Riley, was a lawyer and Greenfield's first mayor. His mother, Elizabeth, occasionally wrote poems published in local newspapers.

Young Jim loved music, theater and art as well as the great outdoors. But he certainly wasn't the best student in his classroom. His father was disappointed when it became obvious that Jim never would be a lawyer, so his he helped Jim find a job as a sign painter.

Sort of a young drifter, Jim Riley wrote jingles and verse. He traveled with a medicine wagon; while a "doc" sold lotions and potions, young Jim entertained the crowds with stories. Eventually, he started writing for a newspaper in Anderson. Then his poetry came to national attention.

The Hoosier Poet settled in the Lockerbie neighborhood of Indianapolis. (James Whitcomb Riley had a pet dog, a white poodle, that he also named Lockerbie.) He never married or had children, but lived for about thirty years in a Lockerbie home owned by friends. In an unusual arrangement, Mr. Riley was a permanent "paying guest."

Riley based some of his most famous poems on people or places he remembered from his boyhood. For example, Riley based "Little Orphant Annie" on a homeless young girl named Mary Alice Smith. In 1862 when

Jim as thirteen, his family took in Mary Alice. She tended house for the Rileys to earn her meals. Before bedtime at night, Mary Alice fascinated Jim and his brothers and sisters by telling them frightening stories.

In "Little Orphant Annie," the character says:

> *You better mind yer parents, an' yer*
> *teachers fond an' dear,*
> *An' cherish them 'at loves you, an' dry*
> *the orphan's tear,*
> *An' he'p the pore an' needy ones 'at*
> *clusters all about,*
> *Er the Gobble-uns'll git you*
> *Ef you*
> *Don't*
> *Watch*
> *Out!*

Riley was invited to the White House to read his poems; his close friends included many of the famous Hoosiers of his time such as Speedway founder Carl Fisher and labor leader Eugene V. Debs.

During one of Riley's performances in Greenfield, so many people were crammed into the Masonic Hall that old-timers worried that the building would collapse when audience members cheered and stomped their feet.

Today, his poetry is still appreciated in his home state and beyond. It recalls a time when life seemed simpler, when people enjoyed unrushed lives. Children roamed the fields and woodlands with friends; neighbors

Beloved Hoosier poet James Whitcomb Riley. (Indiana Historical Society)

in small towns paid attention to each other's problems. This sense of the values of village life in Indiana—of caring about others and loving the home and the great outdoors—was what made Riley's poetry memorable in his own time. These values, along with Riley's skill with words and his taste for fun, keep his poetry fresh.

Despite his wealth and fame—and the sunny outlook of many of his poems—Riley had his share of struggles. He periodically battled loneliness and drinking problems. But he also charmed people of all ages, from millions of Americans who loved his poetry to neighborhood children in Lockerbie. One of them was Agnes Search Bridgford, whose father owned the general store where Riley bought his cigars.

"He'd also buy Kis-Me chewing

gum for us kids," Agnes recalled years later. "Mr. Riley would buy the gum from my father. Then he would drop it on the grassy knoll near Lockerbie Street and tell us children, 'That gum grows there, you know' . . .

"Of course, we knew gum didn't grow on the grass, but it tickled us to hear Mr. Riley say it. Sometimes he even dropped Lincoln pennies on the ground for us."

On the poet's sixty-sixth birthday in 1915, President Woodrow Wilson sent a message paying tribute to "the many pleasures Riley has given me, along with the rest of the great body of readers of English."

Six months later, Mr. Riley died in his sleep at his Lockerbie home. Thirty-five thousand mourners filed past his casket at the Indiana Statehouse. In one of many ways that Hoosiers honored the children's poet, several of his friends founded the Riley Hospital for Children.

Others in the "Big Four" of Indiana literature

James Whitcomb Riley was considered one of a famous "Big Four" group of writers during the Golden Age of Indiana literature in the early 1900s. The other three Hoosiers were **Booth Tarkington** (see his separate section for more information about him), **George Ade**, and **Meredith Nicholson**. All four Hoosiers became well known across the country for the excellence of their poetry, novels, plays, or fables.

George Ade

George Ade (1866–1944) of Kentland, Indiana, wrote plays and modern fables. His fables were moral tales that used everyday language. One of his tales was called *The Fable of the Good People Who Rallied to the Support of the Church*. In it, George Ade described the effort and expense to which congregation members went to decorate for a raspberry festival. When the hoopla was over, the church had raised six dollars and eighty cents. Ade concluded by noting that some people will do anything to avoid putting money in an offering basket.

The tale was included in Ade's first book, *Fables in Slang* (1899), which became a best seller.

George Ade lived on a beautiful estate in northern Indiana called Hazelden. The estate and its elaborate gardens became the setting for parties attended by celebrities such as President Theodore Roosevelt.

Meredith Nicholson

Meredith Nicholson (1866–1947) advised young writers to "stay in your hometown." In his case, there were two: **Crawfordsville**, where he was born, and **Indianapolis**, where he became a politician and served on the Indianapolis City Council in the late 1920s.

Meredith Nicholson usually wrote about Indiana, almost always with great affection. His books included *The Hoosiers*, a cultural history of Indiana published in 1900. In the 1930s and early '40s, Nicholson, a Democrat, served as a diplomat to Paraguay, Venezuela, and Nicaragua.

Theodore Dreiser and Paul Dresser

About the same time that the "Big Four" were making a name for themselves, two brothers from a poor Indiana family also became famous for their works in literature and the arts. They were novelist **Theodore Dreiser** and his older brother, **Paul Dresser**, who composed popular songs such as "On the Banks of the Wabash, Far Away." (It was chosen as Indiana's official state song in 1913, seven years after Dresser died.)

The brothers were two of thirteen children in a loud, rowdy family in

Terre Haute named Dreiser. (Paul changed his name as a young man because he thought "Dresser" would be easier for people to remember.) Three of the ten children in the poverty-stricken Dreiser family died as babies.

Soon after the birth of Theodore (1871–1945), who was the ninth child, their father lost his job. The family moved to a series of Indiana towns, many of them near the Wabash River (which Paul loved and later featured in his songs). As they struggled to survive, several family members developed drinking problems. The wild-living Dreiser family often was the target of town gossip.

Paul (1858–1906) and Theodore separately moved to the big city of Chicago as young men. Theodore entered the hardscrabble world of Chicago newspapers, becoming a reporter. He wrote about miserable big-city living and working conditions during the "Industrial Revolution" in his most famous books, including *Sister Carrie* (1900). Theodore Dreiser also wrote about the unhappiness of the wealthy—as well as the problems of people who will do almost anything to become rich. Those are the themes of one of his classic novels, *An American Tragedy* (1925).

In contrast, Paul Dresser's music often is perky, soothing, or homey.

Consider the chorus of "On the Banks of the Wabash, Far Away," which includes these lines:

Oh, the moonlight's fair tonight along the Wabash,
From the fields there comes the breath of new-mown hay.
Through the sycamores the candle lights are gleaming,
On the banks of the Wabash, far away.

Even though "On the Banks of the Wabash" didn't become the state song until 1913, Paul Dresser wrote it in 1897. One of his other popular tunes, "My Gal Sal" (1905), is a favorite of barbershop quartets to this day.

Theodore Dreiser, novelist. (Courtesy of Vigo County Historical Society)

Booth Tarkington

Penrod Schofield was a mischievous twelve-year-old boy living in **Indian-apolis** during the World War I era (1914–1916). He was created by author **Booth Tarkington**, who based Penrod's adventures on the real-life antics of Tarkington's three nephews. Boys in 1914 enjoyed many of the same activities that they do today—from mud fights and teasing girls to gorging on cookies.

They also loved animals, some-times a bit too much. Penrod and his buddies, Sam and Herman, wanted a cat. They were able to capture a really huge, skinny cat—"part panther or something." They named the big cat Whitney and wanted to keep him.

Penrod knew his parents would object, though. So they hid Whitney in a stable near their house. Then Penrod, Sam and Herman sneaked food from the kitchen, took it to the stable and fed the secret cat.

Here's what Whitney gobbles up in *Penrod and Sam* (1916), one of the Penrod series of books by Tarkington:

Whitney now ate nine turnips, two heads of lettuce, one cabbage, eleven raw potatoes, and the loaf of bread . . .

"Well, sir, I guess we got him filled up at last!" said Penrod. "I bet he

Booth Tarkington, novelist. (Booth Tarkington collection of the Indiana Historical Society)

wouldn't eat a saucer of ice-cream now, if we'd give it to him!"

"He looks better to me," said Sam, staring critically at Whitney. "I think he's kind of begun to fill out some." . . .

"Penrod," said his mother, "what did you do with that loaf of bread Della says you took from the table?"

"Ma'm? What loaf of bread?"

So who was this author who created the kid named Penrod, the cat named Whitney, and all of the other characters? A novelist and playwright, **Booth Tarkington** (1869–1946) was probably the most famous resident of Indianapolis for more than thirty years.

Tarkington won the most distinguished award for writing in America—the Pulitzer Prize—not just once, but twice. He was awarded the Pulitzer Prize for *The Magnificent Ambersons* (1918) and *Alice Adams* (1921), novels about changes in society.

But Tarkington, who lived in a splendid, art-filled mansion on North Meridian Street, was just as well known for his novels about children. In particular, he was famous for his humorous books about Penrod, which began with *Penrod* (1914). The three nephews whose adventures helped inspire the books grew up across the street from their celebrity uncle.

Despite Tarkington's fame and success, his personal life included periods of deep sadness. Tarkington married twice (he divorced his first wife in 1911); his daughter died tragically at age sixteen, and he suffered from eye problems so severe that he nearly was blind for many years. After several operations, Tarkington partially regained his vision near the end of his life.

Even when he barely could see, though, Tarkington never stopped writing. In fact, he took pride in writing every single day of the week.

He is buried in Crown Hill Cemetery near the grave of poet James Whitcomb Riley.

An excerpt from *Penrod*

The Penrod books are considered among the best novels ever written about boyhood in the Midwest. Here's a passage from *Penrod* (1914) about a rowdy neighborhood fight:

Thus began the Great Tar Fight, the origin of which proved, afterward, so difficult for parents to trace, owing to the opposing accounts of the combatants. Marjorie said Penrod began it. Penrod said Mitchy-Mitch began it . . .

Mr. Schofield's version of things was that Penrod was insane. "He's a stark, raving lunatic!" the father declared, descending to the library from a before-dinner interview with the outlaw that evening. "I'd send him to military school, but I don't believe they'd take him. Do you know why he says all that awfulness happened?"

"When Margaret and I were to scrub him," Mrs. Schofield responded wearily, "he said everybody had been calling him names."

"Names!" her husband snorted. " 'Little gentleman'! That's the vile epithet they called him! And because of it, he wrecks the peace of six homes!"

Cole Porter

What is this thing called love?
    This funny thing called love?
Just who can solve its mystery?
    Why should it make a fool of me?
I saw you there one wonderful day.
    You took my heart and threw it away.
That's why I ask the Lord in heaven
    above,
    What is this thing called love?

Those song lyrics were written by—and the music that accompanied them was composed by—a famous Hoosier. Many musicians consider Cole Porter to have been a genius.

In addition to composing "What Is This Thing Called Love?" Cole Porter (1891–1964) wrote dozens of other popular songs that likely will continue to be enjoyed around the world one hundred years from now.

To millions of people, Porter tunes such as "Let's Do It, Let's Fall In Love," are as romantic as Broadway show music ever gets. The Hoosier composer also wrote songs for sophisticated movies that represented the height of glamour, elegance and charm.

All of those qualities figured in the life of Cole Porter, who grew up in a family mansion near Peru, Indiana. Yet this short, frail man also struggled for years with terrible pain and sadness.

Cole Porter, composer and lyricist, wrote the music and the words to dozens of popular songs. (Courtesy of the Miami County Historical Society Inc.)

Cole Porter's cousin, James Cole, at the family mansion near Peru, Indiana, in 1991. (Courtesy of *The Indianapolis Star*)

His legs were crushed in a horseback-riding accident at the peak of his fame in the 1930s. After many unsuccessful treatments, Porter's right leg was amputated in 1958. The composer plunged into a depression and never wrote another song.

Before that, though, his days often were as joyous as his best music. As a boy, he lived near Peru at Westleigh, the nine-hundred-acre estate owned by the Cole family, his mother's relatives. They had become wealthy by owning lumber mills and large areas of land.

In 1902, when Porter was only eleven years old, his mother arranged for the publication of one of his music compositions, "The Bobolink Waltz." That was the start of a spectacular career. At Yale University, where Cole attended college, he wrote his first hit. It was the school's famous football fight song, "Yale Bulldog," which is still sung on campus to this day at the famed university in Connecticut.

Cole Porter enjoyed a remarkable string of hit musicals on the Broadway stage such as *Anything Goes* (1934) and *Kiss Me Kate* (1948). His show tunes included one of his most celebrated songs, "Night and Day." He alternated his Broadway work with composing for Hollywood movie musicals, including films that starred the dance team of Fred Astaire and Ginger Rogers. One of his many popular songs written for a movie was "In The Still of the Night":

> In the still of the night
>   As I gaze out my window
> At the moon in its flight
>   My thoughts all stray to you.
> In the still of the night,
>   While the world is in slumber,
> Oh, the times without number,
>   Darling, when I say to you,
> 'Do you love me as I love you?
>   Are you my life-to-be, my
>   dream come true?'
> Or will this dream of mine
>   Fade out of sight
> Like the moon
>   Growing dim

> On the rim
>   Of the hill
> In the chill,
>   Still of the night.

Porter wrote that song in 1937. That same year, he was thrown from a horse, which then fell on top of him, crushing his legs. The composer endured about thirty-five operations and remained in constant agony.

Although he lived lavishly in apartments all over the world—New York, London and Paris—Cole Porter frequently returned to Indiana to visit his mother, Kate, at Westleigh. In the early 1950s, he was devastated by her death and, two years later, the death of his wife, Linda. Then came the amputation of his leg.

"He became a recluse," his cousin, James Cole, recalled in an interview.

But isn't it wonderful this brilliant composer created music that still lifts the spirits of millions of people when they listen to it?

The lyrics to "You're the Top"

When it comes to popular American composers, Cole Porter is at the very top. So isn't it appropriate that he wrote a song called "You're the Top"?

In the lyrics, he compares the object of his devotion to the world's most famous buildings, paintings, clothes, music, rivers—even to a famous cartoon character.

> You're the top!
>   You're the Colosseum
> You're the top!
>   You're the Louvre Museum
> You're a melody from a symphony by Strauss
>   You're a Bendel bonnet,
> A Shakespeare sonnet,
>   You're Mickey Mouse!
> You're the Nile,
>   You're the Tower of Pisa,
> You're the smile
>   On the Mona Lisa
> I'm a worthless check, a total wreck, a flop,
>   But, if baby, I'm the bottom
> You're the top!

(The Louvre is a museum in Paris, France, that has several of the world's most famous oil paintings, including the Mona Lisa. The Colosseum is a magnificent structure built by the ancient Romans. And the Nile is the longest river in the world.)

Hoagy Carmichael

According to some accounts, a dreamy-sounding tune called "Stardust" has the distinction of being the most recorded song in the world. Its composer, **Hoagy Carmichael** of **Bloomington**, Indiana, certainly was no one-hit wonder. This remarkable songwriter composed about fifty hit tunes and has been called "Hollywood's first piano man" because he portrayed himself (or piano-playing characters like himself) in several movies.

Most of his hit songs are jazz tunes with a dreamy quality. They include "Georgia On My Mind," "Up A Lazy River," "The Nearness of You," and "Lazy Bones." For "In The Cool, Cool, Cool of the Evening," Carmichael won the Academy Award for Best Song in 1951.

Several of Carmichael's songs were based on people or places in Indiana. "Rockin' Chair," a song he wrote in 1929, was inspired by an elderly African-American resident of Bloomington. That's where Hoagland Howard "Hoagy" Carmichael was born in 1899.

Even as a small boy, Hoagy was fascinated by music. His mother was a pianist who performed in movie theaters; her job was to play music to accompany silent movies. Other than the musical instruction that young

Legendary composer Hoagy Carmichael was popular in radio (as shown here), TV, and the movies. (Photofest)

Other legends in Jazz music from Indiana

Wes Montgomery

Wes Montgomery, jazz guitarist.
(Indiana Historical Society)

From the 1940s through the mid-1960s, the diagonal street of Indiana Avenue in Indianapolis was the center of a thriving jazz scene. For much of that period, the key musician in jazz along "The Avenue" was Wes Montgomery, a guitarist. He became internationally known as one of the most innovative guitarists of the twentieth century.

Amazingly, this famous Hoosier—who was named John Leslie Montgomery at his birth in 1923—didn't even pick up a guitar until he was nineteen years old and married.

His late start—and the fact that Wes Montgomery taught himself how to play—didn't matter. In the late 1940s, Montgomery joined the Lionel Hampton Trio and toured the country. He also became a popular headliner at the clubs along Indiana Avenue in his hometown. With his brothers Monk and Buddy, he released his first recording, *The Wes Montgomery Trio*, in 1959. Successes kept coming. In 1965, Montgomery's album *Goin' Out of My Head* won a Grammy Award.

As he was preparing to tour Japan in 1968, Wes Montgomery died of a heart attack; he was only forty-five years old. A jazz festival and a park in Indianapolis are named in his honor.

David Baker

David Baker (left) prepares to perform at a jazz festival in Indianapolis. (Stephen Baker)

Indianapolis also is the hometown of David Baker (born in 1932), who has made an impact as a performer, composer and teacher. As he was growing up, David Baker was influenced by Wes Montgomery. Like the hometown musician he respected, David Baker went on to play in Lionel Hampton's jazz band.

Since 1966, David Baker has been a professor at the Indiana University School of Music, where he heads the jazz department. He's credited with pioneering the use of cellos in jazz.

David Baker has composed music played by the Indianapolis Symphony Orchestra, and he conducted the first orchestra funded by the Smithsonian Institution in Washington, D.C.

Hoagy received from his mother, he never took formal lessons.

However, he picked up plenty of musical tips as a teenager by hanging around jazz and ragtime piano players, particularly African-American musicians. The early 1900s was an era of racial segregation, when most whites and blacks lived in separate neighborhoods. Even so, skinny young Hoagy was warmly invited into the homes of black musicians in Indianapolis and Bloomington, as the Carmichael family alternated between living in the two cities.

Carmichael particularly admired the music of Reggie DuValle, a ragtime piano player. In his Indianapolis home, Reggie DuValle showed "the kid" how to improvise on the keyboard. (Reggie DuValle's piano now is exhibited at the Indiana Historical Society in downtown Indianapolis.)

When Hoagy Carmichael was a student at Indiana University in the 1920s, he formed a band called The Collegians. Even though he was studying law at IU, his passion was music, and he often could be found at a Greek-owned candy and malt store off campus called The Book Nook. The shop had a piano in the back room, and he began composing tunes on it, including "Washboard Blues," "Riverboat Shuffle," and "Rockin' Chair."

In the late 1920s, Hoagy wrote the music and early versions of the lyrics (words) for "Stardust." Initially, he composed the song with a fast tempo, and "Stardust" was not particularly popular. But in 1930, "Stardust" became a huge hit when orchestras recorded it in a slow, dreamy style. In less than ten years, "Stardust" sold one million copies and brought Hoagy Carmichael fame for the rest of his life.

Show business became his world. His first movie role was as "Cricket," a piano player, in *To Have and Have Not* (1944). The lingering image of Hoagy for most people is the way he came across in the movie *Canyon Passage* (1946). In the film, thin-faced Hoagy puts on a top hat, rides a mule and warbles his song, "Old Buttermilk Sky." The movie that featured the Oscar-winning song "In the Cool, Cool, Cool of the Evening" was a musical called *Here Comes the Groom*.

Carmichael's other songs included "Can't Get Indiana Off My Mind."

"It's people like Dad who, in my opinion, helped make Hoosiers feel comfortably at home in Indiana," says Randy Carmichael, Hoagy's youngest son. (His other son is named Hoagland Bix Carmichael.)

Hoagy Carmichael died in 1981, but his music is played somewhere around the world every day. "Georgia On My Mind" is continually recorded by newly popular performers—including jazz great Ray Charles and pop star Michael Bolton.

In 1971, Carmichael was inducted into the Songwriters Hall of Fame.

Kurt Vonnegut Jr.

One of today's most famous novelists grew up in Indianapolis and graduated from Shortridge High School.

Kurt Vonnegut Jr.—who is easy to recognize because of his mustache, frizzy hair, and biting humor—was born in Indianapolis in 1922. By then, his family had been prominent in the city's affairs for many years.

His grandfather, who had been born in Germany, was an architect. He designed the Athenaeum, a majestic building in downtown Indianapolis that for years was a meeting and party hall for German Americans. Thousands of Hoosiers still use the Athenaeum that way, as well as for its theater and restaurant. Kurt Jr.'s father, Kurt Sr., was an architect, too. The family also owned hardware stores in Indianapolis.

"Indianapolis made me what I am today," Kurt Jr. says. "The city was a terrific influence. Of course, my parents and most of my relatives were well-educated people, so their houses were full of books and music. I could not have done better for myself."

Does that sound cheerful and optimistic? Well, that's not usually how Vonnegut comes across—in person or in his writing. He's experienced periods of deep sadness and even horror during his life; that shows up in many of his best-selling novels.

Novelist Kurt Vonnegut Jr.
(Photofest)

As a soldier during World War II (1941–1945), Vonnegut was captured and held in Germany as a prisoner of war. He witnessed a bombing raid that destroyed the German city of Dresden and killed thousands of people.

Several of the novels that Vonnegut wrote years later—including *Cat's Cradle* (1963) and *Slaughterhouse-Five* (1969)—have strong anti-war themes. Some of his books, including *Breakfast of Champions* (1973), also have Hoo-siers as characters—and the author pokes fun at them.

It's certainly safe to say that Vonnegut has had a love-hate relationship with his home state over the years. For most of his writing career, he has lived in the New York City area. Periodically, he returns to Indianapolis for speeches and awards, though. In 1999, the Indiana Historical Society named him a "Living Legend."

Another Indiana writer of today: Dan Wakefield

A book published in 1996 is dedicated to several Hoosiers, including teachers and librarians. The author of *Creating from the Spirit: Living Each Day as a Creative Act* is Indianapolis native Dan Wakefield. The book celebrates people who take creative approaches to their jobs, whether they are secretaries, chefs, ministers, architects or telephone operators.

So why did Dan Wakefield dedicate the book to Indianapolis teachers and librarians?

"They helped inspire my creativity," says Wakefield, who was born in 1932. He contends that anyone who takes a fresh, lively approach to work or play is being creative.

In recent years, Dan Wakefield has carved out a second career as a leader of creativity workshops and spiritual workshops where people explore their religious faith. His recent books have included *Expect a Miracle* (1995), which consists of interviews with people who feel their lives have been changed by miracles, and *The Story of Your Life: Writing A Spiritual Autobiography* (1990).

What, then, was his first career?

After graduating from Shortridge High School in 1950 (where his classmates included future U.S. Senator Richard Lugar), Dan Wakefield moved to New York City. He became a magazine writer and the author of *Going All the Way* (1970), a best-selling novel set in Indianapolis during the 1950s. Dan Wakefield also struggled with alcoholism, and has written candidly about his painful recovery. Religious experiences played a role in his healing, although Dan Wakefield does not describe himself as having been "born-again."

Author Dan Wakefield enjoys seeing former classmates at the reunion of his Shortridge High School class in 1985. (Courtesy of *The Indianapolis Star*)

"I like to describe myself as 'turning,' which is a continual, gradual process," he says. "What I talk about is a constant journey, like walking along a road."

Fun facts about Kurt Vonnegut Jr.

- In his novels and short stories, Kurt Vonnegut, Jr., frequently describes the crazy behavior—and cruelty—of human beings. One of his most popular books, a collection of short stories, is called *Welcome to the Monkey House* (1968).

- Vonnegut was in awe of his older brother, Bernard, a scientist. Bernard Vonnegut became one of the world's top experts on—hold onto your hat—tornadoes. He died in 1997 at age eighty-two.

Robert Indiana and LOVE

"Love is all around," or so the song says. In the case of **Robert Indiana**, it's true! There are LOVE paperweights, posters, key chains and coffee mugs. All of those are spin-offs of the original famous *LOVE* images: a *LOVE* painting and sculpture at the Indianapolis Museum of Art. Robert Indiana, a Hoosier artist, created the painting and sculpture.

He was named Robert Clark when he was born in **New Castle** in 1928. But the painter and sculptor eventually had his name legally changed to Robert Indiana as a tribute to his home state.

Before Clark/Indiana turned seventeen, his family had moved twenty-one times. Even so, he spent most of his youth in the Indianapolis area. His artistic talents became apparent at Arsenal Technical High School. (While he was enrolled at Tech, he also studied at the Herron School of Art.)

Always fascinated by signs, logos, and symbols, Robert Indiana eventually studied art in Chicago, England, and Scotland. Since 1978, he has lived in seclusion on a small island off the coast of Maine.

His *LOVE* sculpture—one of the world's most famous pop art images—stands on the front lawn of the Indianapolis Museum of Art. You can't

Three seasons of *LOVE*: Robert Indiana's world-famous sculpture at the Indianapolis Museum of Art in winter, summer, and fall. The artist also created a *LOVE* painting. (Indianapolis Museum of Art, Gift of the Friends of the IMA in memory of Henry F. DeBoest)

miss it during any visit to the museum: It's near the entrance.

In recent years, Robert Indiana has been creating a mammoth sculpture— an artwork more than fifty feet tall. It is for the new Indiana State Museum in White River State Park.

Twyla Tharp

A choreographer is a dance director and creator. One of the country's most famous choreographers and dancers, **Twyla Tharp**, was born in **Portland**, Indiana, in 1941.

Tharp's family had been Quaker farmers in Jay County for five generations. In Portland, Twyla began piano lessons at two and dance training at four. But she moved with her parents to southern California when she was eight years old.

Her extraordinary talents as a dancer and choreographer resulted in performances around the world. Twyla Tharp has created dances for everyone from the Joffrey Ballet to professional ice dancers. She also has choreographed scenes for several movies. They include *Amadeus* (1984), which tells the story of Mozart, the classical music composer; and *White Knights* (1985), which starred Mikhail Baryshnikov, one of the most famous dancers in the world. Paired with Baryshnikov, Tharp toured across the country in the 1990s; they performed in concerts in Indiana.

During her career, Twyla Tharp has won dozens of top medals and awards, including an Emmy Award in 1985 for a TV special.

Fun fact: According to Twyla Tharp, she was named after Twila Thornburg, the reigning Pig Princess at a Muncie fair.

Religious and Spiritual Figures

Mother Theodore Guerin

She wasn't a typical pioneer.

Mother Theodore Guerin of France was a Catholic nun in frail health. She could eat only soft, bland food. And Mother Theodore was not young: She was nearly forty-two years old in 1840 when she arrived in the Indiana wilderness to start a religious community, schools and orphanages.

Yet her achievements in the frontier were so remarkable that Mother Theodore (1798–1856) may be designated a saint by the Roman Catholic Church.

"What strength the soul draws from prayer!" Mother Theodore wrote after surviving a horrible storm in the Atlantic Ocean during her voyage to the young land of America. "In the midst of a storm, how sweet is the calm it (prayer) finds in the heart of Jesus."

Mother Theodore was named Anne-Therese Guerin when she was born in the little French village of Étables-sur-Mer. She apparently always felt drawn to a life of serving God. When she was in her twenties, Anne-Therese became a nun. She took the name Sister Theodore and joined the Sisters of Providence, a community of nuns in France who were teachers and cared for the poor and sick.

In 1839, Mother Theodore was asked to be in charge of five other nuns

Mother Theodore Guerin, founder of Catholic schools and an Indiana pioneer. (Courtesy of Saint Mary-of-the-Woods)

from the Sisters of Providence who would travel to the Indiana frontier. Their tasks were to found a convent and schools and to bring religion to pioneers near the community of **Vincennes**.

Traveling by ship, steamboat, train and horse-drawn carriage, Mother Theodore and the others arrived at their settlement—what became **Saint Mary-of-the-Woods** in the forests of western Indiana—in October 1840. The settlement consisted only of a log cabin (it would serve as the chapel) and a small farmhouse where the French nuns lived.

"Imagine our astonishment at finding ourselves in the midst of the forest, no village, and not even a home in sight," Mother Theodore wrote in her journal. "Walking a short distance down a hill, we beheld through the trees on the other side of the ravine a log house with a shed in the rear."

The shed became the nuns' kitchen. One large room in the log farmhouse served as a dormitory, recreation room and infirmary. During their first winter, the nuns frequently were cold, hungry and exhausted.

The Indiana winter was hard and long. In spring, the nuns—along with a few workmen from neighboring communities—cleared the grounds and continued building an academy building, roads and walkways. They also laid out gardens. All of this work was done under the supervision of Mother Theodore; in many cases, Mother Theodore and the other nuns did the heavy work themselves, even though they were not used to farming or manual labor.

Yet within a year, Mother Theodore had opened an academy for girls, which today is Saint Mary-of-the-Woods College. (It is now the oldest Catholic liberal arts college for women in the nation.) The first students were admitted in July 1841. Then Mother Theodore began founding schools in **Jasper**, **Vincennes**, **Madison**, and other Indiana towns.

She established two orphanages in Vincennes—one for boys, the other for girls. Mother Theodore also opened frontier versions of pharmacies (drugstores) that gave free medicine to the poor.

By the time Mother Theodore died in 1856, she had started schools in cities all over Indiana—from Fort Wayne to Columbus, Terre Haute and Evansville.

In 1998—more than 140 years after her death—Mother Theodore was beatified by Pope John Paul II, a step toward sainthood in the Catholic Church. If that happens, she would become only the fourth North American saint.

Reverend Theodore Hesburgh

The Guinness Book of World Records lists thousands of interesting records—about people who have jumped rope for hours, danced for days or stuffed themselves on pie. **Reverend Theodore Hesburgh** of **South Bend** is featured in the *Guinness Book*, too—and for something a lot more distinguished than jumping rope or eating pie. Father Hesburgh has received more honorary degrees from universities—144 degrees, in fact—than anyone else in the world.

For more than fifty years, Father Hesburgh has been one of the most famous Catholics in the United States. The dynamic, silver-haired priest—an adviser to presidents and popes—became known as "Mr. Notre Dame" because he served as president of the University of Notre Dame longer than anyone else: thirty-five years (1952–1987). In fact, when Father Hesburgh retired, he had been in his job longer than had any other college president in America.

Father Hesburgh, who was born in 1917, is almost as well known for his human rights work around the world as he is for his accomplishments at Notre Dame. For decades, he crusaded for world peace and fought against hunger and poverty. He served several years as

Reverend Theodore Hesburgh, the legendary president of the University of Notre Dame. (Courtesy of *The Indianapolis Star*)

president of the U.S. Commission on Civil Rights.

Father Hesburgh has visited more than a hundred and thirty countries. In the early 1960s, he even celebrated Mass among penguins on the South Pole. (Father Hesburgh, a science buff, had joined a twenty-four-man expedition to Antarctica.)

"No matter who you are, he speaks your language," says Reverend Edward Malloy, the priest who followed Hesburgh as president of Notre Dame. He's referring to Hesburgh's ability to relate to everyone—from the heads of big companies to secretaries, custodians and, of course, young people.

"The best young people I know today are giving something back," Father Hesburgh says. "They work with handicapped children. They tutor. They work in soup kitchens."

During most of "the Hesburgh era" at Notre Dame, the famous priest has lived in a barren room on campus that overlooks a trash bin. That's because he is a priest; he has vowed to live in poverty, chastity, and obedience. That means Father Hesburgh and other priests don't marry and don't acquire many possessions so they can focus their energy and attention on their spiritual beliefs and on serving others.

Fun facts

- In 2000, Father Hesburgh received the Congressional Gold Medal, the highest honor that Congress can award to an American citizen.

- When Ann Landers, the famous advice columnist, needed comfort during her divorce, she turned to Father Hesburgh, her old friend. He has comforted and advised dozens of famous Americans that way.

- Although Father Hesburgh has lived in South Bend for most of his life, he didn't start out as a Hoosier. He was born in Syracuse, New York.

- Notre Dame is probably the best-known American university affiliated with the Catholic Church. There are about 10,300 students on the campus in South Bend; about half are Catholics, but students of all faiths are welcome to apply.

- In 1972, Father Hesburgh opened the university to women. Previously, Notre Dame had admitted only men.

Sandi Patty

Blessed with a soaring singing voice, Anderson resident Sandi Patty has soared to the very top with one of the most extraordinary careers in contemporary Christian music. She has sung at the nation's largest cathedrals, at the White House and at the Miss America pageant. She has won five Grammy Awards and an extraordinary thirty-nine Dove Awards. She has made five gold albums and three platinum albums.

When the Statue of Liberty celebrated its one hundredth birthday in 1986, it was Sandi Patty's rendition of the national anthem—"The Star-Spangled Banner"—that was featured on national TV coverage of the ceremonies.

Yet Sandi says her most important job is being a mother to her blended family of eight children in Anderson, where she has continued to live after achieving world fame. Her albums, including *Mornings Like This* and *Another Time . . . Another Place*, have sold several million copies around the world.

Sandi didn't start out a Hoosier. She was born in Oklahoma City, Oklahoma, in 1956. Her parents were gospel musicians. Little Sandi sang her first church solo when she was two-and-a-half years old.

Sandi Patty, Grammy Award-winning gospel singer. (Atkinson-Muse Public Relations)

She has often recalled her father's musical advice: "Make every minute of a song be worth something."

Patty moved to Indiana in the mid-1970s to attend Anderson University. That's where she met Bill and Gloria Gaither, famous Hoosier gospel singers who would change her life. Gaither made Sandi a member of the Bill Gaither Trio. Spectacular success followed. The Gospel Music Association named Sandi Patty the top female vocalist of the year eleven straight times.

Her life also has included deep sadness. Patty and her first husband were involved in a messy divorce, which caused some of her fans to lose interest in her. And some of her children have struggled with severe health problems. One of her sons had to undergo brain surgery.

In 1985, her infant daughter Anna—not yet one year old—nearly died after having a severe reaction to medication. Patty was in the midst of a heavy touring schedule; after every concert, she flew to the hospital to be with Anna until she recovered. Five years later, an arson fire at her headquarters in Anderson destroyed four of her five Grammy Awards.

"The struggles seem to put things into perspective and help me realize that of all the things that grab for my attention on a daily basis, it is my faith, my friends and my family that hold the true importance," she said in *Storms of Perfection*, a book about the challenges faced by famous Americans.

In 1995, she married her second husband, Don Peslis. Sandi Patty resumed touring, and she frequently sings at major events in her adopted home state—from the Indianapolis 500 race and the 1991 World Gymnastics Championships to Christmas concerts with the Indianapolis Symphony Orchestra.

Other Indiana legends in religion

Billy Sunday

He was probably the most famous American evangelist (traveling preacher) in the United States during the World War I era of the late 1910s.

Billy Sunday (1862–1935) grew up in Iowa. During most of his preaching years, he was based in Chicago. But in 1911 he settled for part of each year at a home in **Winona Lake** in northern Indiana. At Winona Lake today, there is a major Christian campground with a large Billy Sunday Tabernacle in the center. Bill Sunday's home, which he called Mount Hood, still stands there. It's now called the Billy Sunday House Museum and has many of his belongings on display—including his reading glasses, books and a grandfather clock given to him by grateful people who participated in his religious crusades.

Who exactly was the person born William Ashley Sunday Jr. in Ames, Iowa?

He eventually was many things: an orphan (his father, a Union soldier in the Civil War, died of pneumonia only one month after Billy was born in 1862), a firefighter and even, amazingly, a well-known baseball player. In the 1880s, he was a star outfielder with the Chicago White Stockings (a team that eventually became the Chicago Cubs). As a pro baseball player, Billy Sunday enjoyed partying. According to legend, one day after some partying at taverns with his teammates, he heard a gospel group singing hymns that his mother had sung to him as a child.

"Boys, I bid the old life goodbye," Sunday claimed to have told his teammates.

He played for other baseball teams, but became a full-time evangelist in 1896. Sunday traveled across the country to preach, holding revival meetings in small towns and major cities alike.

He often preached in tents and spoke about the dangers of alcohol.

He visited beautiful Winona Lake because it was a popular spot for Bible conferences in the early 1900s. Sunday preached his last sermon in Mishawaka, Indiana, a few weeks before dying of a heart attack in 1935. During his forty years of delivering sermons, it is estimated that Sunday preached face-to-face to a hundred million people—and to many more as a result of his popular radio shows.

Elton Trueblood

Earlham College is a small, respected college in Richmond that was founded by Quakers. Just as Herman B Wells became known as "Mr. IU" because he was so widely loved at (and devoted to) Indiana University, kindly Elton Trueblood often was referred to as "Mr. Earlham."

Also like Wells, Trueblood (1900–1994) had a remarkably long, active career. Even in his nineties, he lived on campus, worked on books about faith and offered warm, helpful advice to young students.

Trueblood came from a long line of Quakers. (His ancestors in England were thrown in prison for their Quaker beliefs in the 1600s.) He wrote thirty-six books on spiritual topics and ethics—that is, living a moral life. He became a professor at Earlham in 1946 and taught for twenty years.

In Richmond, he founded York-fellow International, a group of community leaders devoted to using their Christian faith in daily life. Although Trueblood stopped teaching in 1966, he continued living on campus and writing for twenty more years. His books include *The Humor of Christ*. Many of his sayings were quoted by newspaper columnists (including "Dear Abby"), preachers and teachers. Here's one of his most famous sayings:

"Man is the only animal who laughs, the only one who weeps, the only one who prays, the only one who can invent, the only one who is proud . . . the only one who is penitent, and the only one who needs to be."

Ask an adult what "penitent" means—then you will understand the point that Elton Trueblood was making so well.

Legends in Communications

Ernie Pyle

The most famous journalist who reported about World War II was a Hoosier born on a farm in southern Indiana. **Ernie Pyle**—a farm boy who grew up near the town of **Dana**—went on to become a hero to millions of Americans for the way he wrote, for the way he risked his life to tell the soldiers' stories and for the way he died.

Pyle (1900–1945) didn't write about generals and admirals in his newspaper columns about World War II. He traveled to the front lines and shivered in foxholes to tell his readers about the struggles of their fighting men. In 1944, Pyle won journalism's highest honor, the Pulitzer Prize, for his columns about American soldiers.

Many of Pyle's reports from the front lines of World War II described the horrors of war. They also described fleeting moments of calm, friendship and warmth.

The GIs loved Ernie Pyle. Like many of them, the Hoosier journalist didn't make it home.

In April of 1945, during the final days of World War II, Pyle was traveling in a jeep with several officers. Suddenly, the group came under fire from a Japanese gunner, and Pyle was killed.

Famous war correspondent Ernie Pyle grew up near Dana, Indiana, in a house without electricity or plumbing. He never forgot his humble roots. (Photofest)

A plaque on the site (the island of
Ie Shima in the Pacific Ocean) reads:

AT THIS SPOT, THE 77TH INFANTRY
DIVISION LOST A BUDDY, ERNIE PYLE,
18 APRIL 1945.

Ernie Pyle lived the life of a soldier during World War II, and was able to
describe what life in combat was really like in his writing. Following is an
excerpt from one of the accounts in his book *Here Is Your War* (Henry Holt &
Co., 1943):

> Army photographers are soldiers who fight with cameras instead of guns.
> They are in the Signal Corps, and their purpose is twofold—to get newsreels
> for showing in the theaters back home and to make a permanent pictorial
> record of the war. There are many of these men, both in the Army and the
> Navy . . . Many of them will die behind their cameras before it is all over . . .
>
> I had been in Africa a few days when I ran into Private Ned Modica . . .
> Ned was thirty-five, and had coal-black hair, slightly graying . . . [He] had
> gone by foot up to the front line of the attack . . . Ned became momentarily
> oblivious to the danger around him, lost in the craftsman's enthusiasm of
> getting his pictures.
>
> As Ned stood rigid, snapping his pictures, he felt someone leaning
> against him. Making conversation, he said, "It's getting pretty hot, isn't it?"
>
> There was no reply, for just at that moment all the soldiers jumped up
> and began to retreat.
>
> The move was on orders from the commander, who was altering the bat-
> tle tactics, but Ned didn't know that at the time.
>
> He said to a chap leaning against him, "Let's get . . . out of here," and
> whirled around to start running. And as he turned, the soldier fell heavily to
> the ground—dead. Modica never knew who had died while leaning against
> him . . .
>
> The next day, [Ned and other cameramen camped] in tiny shelter tents
> pitched in an olive grove, miles out in the country, and waited for the next
> move. That's where I found them.
>
> "Here in Africa is the first place I ever picked an orange from a tree,"
> said Modica.

Jane Pauley

Millions of TV viewers across the country have watched Jane Pauley anchor news programs and interview famous Americans for more than twenty-five years. Most of those viewers probably think of the broadcast journalist from Indianapolis as poised, professional and in control. They might be surprised to learn that pioneer TV newswoman Jane Pauley was terribly shy when she was attending Eastridge and Moorhead elementary schools on the east side of Indianapolis.

Pauley, who was born in 1950 in Methodist Hospital, has thrived in one of the most high-pressure and stressful situations imaginable—appearing on live TV several days every week. Many people would freeze or panic, but Jane Pauley is known for interviewing celebrities and world leaders calmly and with a sense of humor.

Since 1992, she has been seen on millions of TV sets across the country as a co-anchor of *Dateline NBC*, interviewing famous people such as former first lady Hillary Rodham Clinton; Olympic figure skater Nancy Kerrigan, who was clubbed in the knee before competing; and TV star Michael J. Fox.

Pauley has been talking to top newsmakers ever since 1976. That was when the Hoosier made national headlines herself when she replaced super-

Jane Pauley, TV newswoman. (Photofest)

When *The Today Show* came to Indianapolis for a broadcast in 1986, co-host Jane Pauley received a surprise visit from her former Warren Central High School teacher, Harry Wilfong. (Courtesy of *The Indianapolis Star*)

star journalist Barbara Walters on *The Today Show*, the early-morning news program.

As a young girl in Indianapolis, though, Pauley was very timid. She shares an incident that is an example of her onetime shyness: Her full name is Margaret Jane Pauley. So her second-grade teacher assumed that she preferred to be called "Margaret" and referred to her that way on the first day of class. Pauley was too timid to correct her, and for the entire year at school she was called "Margaret."

By the time Pauley attended Warren Central High School, though, she had overcome her shyness. She became a state champion debater and was elected head of Indiana Girls State, a major victory for a Hoosier teenager.

After graduating from Warren Central in 1968, Pauley studied political science at Indiana University. Then she landed TV news anchor jobs at WISH-TV (Channel 8) in Indianapolis and then at a TV station in Chicago. Next came the big time with *The Today Show*, which she cohosted for thirteen years (until 1989), longer than any other woman broadcaster.

Since 1992, Pauley coanchored *Dateline NBC*, a prime-time TV newsmagazine program that is broadcast several times a week. She and her husband, cartoonist Garry Trudeau, are the parents of three children: a set of twins, Ross and Rachel (who were born in 1983 amid much national publicity), and son Thomas (born in 1986).

Their mother says her children sometimes remind her of herself when she was young.

"None of my kids are extroverted (outgoing)," Pauley says. "But they are all kind. That pleases me immensely . . . Part of my role as a parent involves bringing the kindness out. What a relief it already seems to be there."

Fun facts

- Jane Pauley celebrates her birthday every Halloween. She was born on October 31, 1950.
- She is married to a famous cartoonist. Her husband, Garry Trudeau, is the creator of *Doonesbury*, a political comic strip that appears in hundreds of newspapers across the country. Pauley and Trudeau had a famous matchmaker: They were introduced at a dinner party by Tom Brokaw, who is the anchor of *NBC Nightly News*.
- Her hairstyle has changed dozens of times during the twenty-five years that she has been on national TV. She loves to joke about that. "I truly think I invented the phrase 'bad hair day,'" Pauley says.
- With *The Today Show* and *Dateline NBC*, she has reported from all over the world. In the 1980s, Pauley broadcast from South America, covered the weddings of Great Britain's royal family, and reported from the world's largest cruise ship. Just before Easter in 1985, she traveled to Rome and met the pope; that was the first time American TV cameras were permitted inside the pope's private chapel, which was built in the 1400s.

Dr. Nancy Snyderman

Television viewers across the country regularly watch **Dr. Nancy Snyderman**'s reports on medical topics for the ABC News programs *Good Morning, America* and *20/20*. That, though, is only one of the demanding jobs held down by this Hoosier, who is known for her insight and poise. Dr. Snyderman also is a surgeon who specializes in ear, nose and throat procedures. She's a health columnist for *Good House-keeping* and is also a wife and the mother of three children.

Nancy (who was born in 1952) says she wanted to be a doctor ever since her childhood in **Fort Wayne**, where her father, Dr. Sanford Snyderman, was a surgeon. As a kindergartener, she began accompanying him on his rounds at hospitals; as a teenager, Nancy watched her dad quickly save a patient's life with an emergency surgery. That made her more determined than ever to practice medicine.

Now she lives with her family near San Francisco, where she's a surgeon on staff at a medical center. But Snyderman frequently commutes across the country to New York City for her TV jobs. She's been a frequent "substitute host" on *Good Morning, America* since the early 1990s. Primarily, though, she

Dr. Nancy Snyderman, a surgeon and TV correspondent, reports on medical topics for *Good Morning, America* and *20/20*. (Ida Mae Astute, courtesy of ABC-TV News)

is known for her health reports on topics ranging from anorexia (an eating disorder) among young girls to breast cancer in women. Sometimes Nancy even draws on her personal life for her TV medical news; in late 1994, the birth of her youngest son, Charlie, was

broadcast on *Oprah!* and *Good Morning, America*.

"Whether you're talking to a patient at his bedside or to millions of people on TV," she says, "the challenge is to take a complicated message and break it down into a simple, clear one."

Sportscasters from Indiana

Chris Schenkel

"From Bippus to bowling."

That could be a motto for smooth-voiced TV and radio sportscaster **Chris Schenkel**, a graduate of Purdue University. He grew up on his family's farm near the tiny town of **Bippus** in Indiana's far-northeastern corner. Schenkel (1923–) went on to become famous for his broadcasts of pro bowling tournaments.

As one of the best-known sportscasters on national TV in the 1960s and '70s, he traveled around the world to cover everything from the Olympics, football and golf to boxing, horse racing, and rodeo. In fact, Schenkel was there at the very beginnings of televised football. He broadcast one of the first college football games on TV in 1947.

Schenkel and his wife, Fran, live on a farm on the banks of Lake Tippecanoe—about twenty miles from Bippus.

Tom Carnegie

"It's a new track record!"

That famous phrase at the Indianapolis Motor Speedway will forever be associated with **Tom Carnegie**. He's been known as "the voice of the 500" by being the track announcer at the Speedway for more than forty years.

Carnegie (who was born in 1919) dreamed of being an athlete as a boy. But a polio-related virus weakened his legs, so he became a sports announcer. With his rich, booming voice, Carnegie quickly became famous around the state. For years, he announced nearly every major sporting event in Indiana, including the boys' high school basketball tournament.

In May 2001, TV sportscaster Tom Carnegie interviewed race driver Stephan Gregoire during practice for the Indianapolis 500. (Stephen Baker)

Hoosier Entertainment Legends

Golden Age movie stars from Indiana

One of the most glamorous movie stars of the 1930s and '40s grew up as a tomboy in **Fort Wayne**, Indiana. Wise-cracking blond **Carole Lombard** was Hollywood's highest-paid actress at one point in the 1930s. The period from the 1930s through the '50s often is called the "Golden Age of Hollywood" because so many classic movies were made then—and movie stars exuded elegance.

Movie stars like Carole Lombard were placed under contract to various studios. The studios had makeup, publicity, and wardrobe departments, as well as huge sets in southern California that were built to look like everything from small towns to swamps and castles. Major movie stars were treated almost like royalty—none more so than Lombard and her handsome husband, actor Clark Gable. (He even was nicknamed the "King" of Hollywood.)

Tragically, their storybook marriage—and Lombard's life—were cut short.

In January of 1942, during the bleakest period of World War II, she returned to Indiana to raise money for the American cause. At a rally on Monument Circle in Indianapolis, Lombard spoke to a crowd of twelve thousand Hoosiers. She set a record, selling more than $2 million worth of war bonds.

"There is a bond between people, not only of the same kin, but between people who have a common factor of being loyal, aspiring and dedicated to the joint cause of freedom and justice for all people," she said at the Indianapolis airport. "I am a part of you, and you are a part of me, and we are the people. Hoosiers are the people. I will be back, and when I return it will be with words of victory and peace."

Then, Lombard and her mother boarded an airplane to return to Hollywood and Clark Gable. But the plane crashed in the mountains of Nevada, horrifying millions of fans around the world.

They had adored Lombard in screwball comedies such as *My Man Godfrey* (1936) and *Nothing Sacred* (1937). In many of her movies, Carole Lombard wore evening gowns and jewels—quite a change from the scruffy clothes of her girlhood in Fort Wayne, where she was born in 1908. Her real name was Jane Alice Peters; she grew up in a house near the St. Mary's River, where she often fished and swam.

"I was a complete tomboy," she told interviewers years later. "My brothers were my best friends I ever had, and whatever they did, I did— sometimes a little rougher and always to the dismay of my mother."

Upon Lombard's tragic death at age thirty-three, President Franklin D. Roosevelt sent Clark Gable a message that read:

"Carole . . . brought great joy to all who knew her and to millions who knew her only as a great artist. She gave unselfishly of her time and talent to serve her government in peace and in war. She loved her country. She is and always will be a star."

Will Hays

During the "Golden Age of Hollywood," there was a famous national phrase: "Ask the Hays Office." It was an office that the movie industry set up to make certain that films were clean and wholesome. To run the office, Hollywood studio chiefs selected a respected Hoosier, **Will Hays** (1879–1954). The Hays Office was responsible for reading scripts, screening finished movies, and giving films its seal of approval. Without the seal, a movie couldn't be shown at theaters owned by the studios.

"Good taste is good business," Hays said at one point. He ran the office from the 1920s until 1943.

Hays was born in **Sullivan**, a town

This is one of the last photos ever taken of glamorous movie star Carole Lombard, taken at the rally in Indianapolis right before her death. With her is another legendary Hoosier, Will Hays (right). (Bass Photo Company Collection/Indiana Historical Society Library)

Although McQueen's personal life almost always was troubled, he became a big star in action and adventure movies. They included *The Great Escape* (1963), in which his character leads a massive break from a Nazi prison camp during World War II (it's based on a true story), and *The Towering Inferno* (1974), in which he plays a firefighter dealing with a burning skyscraper.

McQueen died of cancer in 1980.

Red Skelton

A comedian from Vincennes with an easy-to-remember name became one of the most popular funny men in the history of show business. Red Skelton (1913–1997) was a star in almost every form of entertainment: radio, TV, movies, the stage, and the circus.

Richard Bernard Skelton was called "Red" because he was the only redhead in a family of four brothers. The boys were poor because their father had died two months before Red was born. To help pay the bills, Red began performing on stage as a boy. He entertained passengers on showboats that traveled the Ohio and Missouri rivers. Next came jobs as a circus clown.

In the 1930s, Skelton became a hit on stages across the country with a doughnut-dunking comedy routine. Years later, he repeated the routine many times in movies and TV shows. Like many of Skelton's skits, the doughnut-dunking routine was a pantomime—that is, he never spoke.

in southern Indiana. A Republican, he served as U.S. Postmaster (the head of the post office) in the 1920s before Hollywood called.

Years later, his son, Will Hays Jr., served as mayor of Crawfordsville.

Steve McQueen

Among the top Hollywood box office stars of the 1960s and '70s was Steve McQueen, a rugged-looking actor who was born in Beech Grove in 1930.

Terrence Steven McQueen (his full name) grew up in what today would be called a "dysfunctional family." His mother had been a teenage runaway and was struggling with a drinking problem when Steve was born. His father, a pilot, abandoned the family when Steve was a baby, and the boy was shuttled around while he was growing up, shifting between his mother's home in the Indianapolis area and his grandparents, who lived on a farm in Missouri.

During the 1940s, Skelton starred in movies and on radio with his own show. His radio characters included "Junior," a "mean widdle kid." As Junior, he introduced an expression that became a national catch phrase in the early '40s: "I dood it." (*I Dood It* even was the title of a movie that starred Skelton in 1943.)

His gentle, goofy comedy next became a huge hit on television. *The Red Skelton Show* enjoyed an amazing run of twenty years, lasting from 1951 to 1971. Red Skelton's comic characters included "Clem Kadiddlehopper," a confused bumpkin, and "Freddie the Freeloader," a hobo who never spoke.

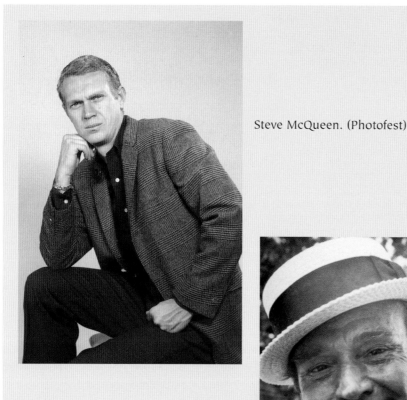

Steve McQueen. (Photofest)

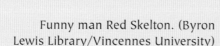

Funny man Red Skelton. (Byron Lewis Library/Vincennes University)

Other "Golden Age" stars

Irene Dunne

She was a singer and actress who earned five Academy Award nominations, although she never won an Oscar. Irene Dunne (1898–1990) grew up in Madison, Indiana, and studied music in Indianapolis. Her most famous films included *Life With Father* (1947), in which she portrayed a patient mother, and *I Remember Mama* (1948), in which she played a beloved Norwegian immigrant.

Clifton Webb

In *Sitting Pretty* (1948), he played a self-centered, harassed baby-sitter. That performance led to a popular series of "Mr. Belvedere" comedies in which Clifton Webb played a fussy, sharp-tongued character. He also played villains in movies such as *Laura* (1948) and even portrayed bandleader John Phillip Sousa, who wrote *Stars and Stripes Forever* (1952). Webb was born in Indianapolis in 1889, but he was only a young boy when he left for New York City with his stage-struck mother. He died in 1966.

Marjorie Main

"Ma and Pa Kettle" were popular hillbilly characters who had fifteen children (!) in a series of "cornpone" comedy movies of the 1940s and '50s.

Marjorie Main, the actress who played "Ma Kettle," was born near Acton, Indiana, in 1890. She grew up in Shelby County, where her father was a minister, and attended Franklin College. Marjorie Main went on to appear in dozens of Broadway plays and movies. Her "Ma Kettle" character first appeared in *The Egg and I* (1947); she was nominated for an Academy Award for her performance. Main's last movie was *The Kettles on Old MacDonald's Farm* (1957). She died in 1975.

Anne Baxter

Every Easter and Passover season, millions of Americans watch the classic movie *The Ten Commandments* (1956). The leading lady is actress **Anne Baxter** (1923–1985) of **Michigan City**, Indiana. She plays Nefertari, the Egyptian princess who loves Moses. Listen to Baxter murmur "Moses, Moses" in her husky voice. Anne Baxter was one of Hollywood's busiest actresses during the 1940s and '50s. Her other movies include *All About Eve* (1950) and *The Fighting Sullivans* (1944), which tells the true story of a family that lost five brothers in World War II; they died fighting side-by-side. Baxter won the Academy Award as Best Supporting Actress in 1946.

Clifton Webb, who played the fussy "Mr. Belvedere." (Photofest)

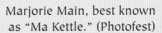

Marjorie Main, best known as "Ma Kettle." (Photofest)

Anne Baxter portrayed the Egyptian princess in love with Moses in the classic 1956 biblical movie *The Ten Commandments*. (Photofest)

"Golden Age" radio and TV stars

The heyday of radio entertainment—comedies, mysteries, quiz shows, and band music—was the 1940s. The next decade, the 1950s, became known as the "Golden Age of TV" because of the booming popularity of television, which captivated millions of Americans. Here are some famous men and women from Indiana who played key roles in both radio and early television:

Phil Harris

To young people, **Phil Harris** of **Linton**, Indiana, is best known as the voice of "Baloo the Bear" in the animated movie *The Jungle Book* (1967). But his major claim to fame was as a bandleader for more than fifty years. Harris (1904–1995) led the bands on several top radio shows, including one that starred comedian Jack Benny. (Harris also played Jack Benny's sidekick on the hugely popular program.) In addition, Harris starred with his wife, glamorous movie star Alice Faye, in a popular radio show from 1946 to 1954. Harris also played himself in several movies. Despite all of his fame, Harris never forgot his Indiana roots. For years—up to and including his ninetieth birthday in 1994—he presided over a celebrity golf tournament and variety show in Linton, a small town in western Indiana near Terre Haute. The Phil Harris Festival raised thousands of dollars for college scholarships for Hoosiers.

Herb Shriner and sons

During the "Golden Age of TV," a comedian from **Fort Wayne** became

Comedian Herb Shriner, known as "the Hoosier Humorist," often played the harmonica in his act. Here he plays with his family (from left): son Wil, who also grew up to be a comedian; wife Pixie; daughter Indiana (called "Indy"); and Wil's twin brother, Kin, future star of *General Hospital* on TV. (Courtesy of *The Indianapolis Star*)

famous as "the Hoosier Humorist." Herb Shriner (1918–1970) played the harmonica and poked gentle fun at Hoosiers on TV variety and game shows, including a quiz show called *Two for the Money*. To tell the truth, Shriner was born in Ohio, not Indiana.

His family moved here when he was just three years old. "I came to Indiana as soon as I heard about it," he used to joke.

In 1953 Shriner became the father of twin sons, Wil and Kin. Legend has it that upon the twins' birth, Herb looked at the nearly identical babies and wisecracked, "Am I supposed to have a choice?" (**Fun fact**: Herb and his wife, Pixie, also had a daughter. They named her "Indiana" out of pride for Herb's adopted state; she lives in California and is nicknamed "Indy.")

Herb and Pixie Shriner were killed in an auto accident in 1970. The children went to live with their grandparents; the twin brothers later entered show business. Like his father, Wil is a comedian. Kin Shriner has starred for many years on *General Hospital*, a long-running daytime soap opera.

Betsy Palmer

A popular TV and movie actress of the 1950s was blond, bubbly **Betsy Palmer** of **East Chicago**, Indiana. She was a panelist for ten years on *I've Got A Secret*, one of TV's longest-running panel shows. (Palmer and other celebrities tried to guess the secrets of various contestants. Sample secret: The movie actor who played the "Frankenstein" monster whispered, "I'm afraid of mice.") Palmer, who was born near East Chicago in 1926, was the leading lady in several dramas on live TV with her close friend, young Hoosier actor James Dean. Palmer's movies included *Mister Roberts* (1955), which is about a World War II cargo ship commanded by a weird captain, and *The Tin Star* (1957), a Western.

Phil Harris: bandleader, radio star, and cartoon voice. (Photofest)

Actress and TV personality Betsy Palmer was a secretary in East Chicago, Indiana, until she took a test that revealed she had a flair for performing. (Photofest)

David Letterman

He's known around the world for his shows featuring "Stupid Pet Tricks" (for one, a man brought his pet duck—which ate cottage cheese from its owner's mouth!) and his popular "Top Ten" lists. But **David Letterman** is on a "Top Fifty" list himself. Right along with famous performers such as Lucille (*I Love Lucy*) Ball, Dave Letterman was named one of the "fifty greatest TV stars of all time" by *TV Guide* magazine.

The wisecracking host of *Late Show with David Letterman* (a late-night talk show that began on CBS-TV in 1993) is so famous that even his mom has become a celebrity. She is Dorothy Letterman Mengering, a white-haired housewife in Carmel, Indiana, who popped up on her son's show with reports from the 1994 Winter Olympics. As a result, she received $1 million to write a cookbook.

Everyone from President George W. Bush to movie star Tom Cruise has taken a seat next to gap-toothed Dave Letterman on his show. He got his start in broadcasting in his hometown—as a TV weatherman for Channel 13 in Indianapolis. Reporting the weather, Letterman couldn't stay serious, amusing viewers—but not always his boss—with goofball humor, once predicting "hail the size of canned hams."

David Letterman at the Indianapolis 500. A big fan of auto racing, Letterman was the co-owner of race driver Bobby Rahal's team for several years in the 1990s. (Stephen Baker)

In the 1980s, Letterman was the host of a late-night talk show on NBC-TV that featured "Stupid Pet Tricks" and "Top Ten" lists. (Photofest)

That was in the early and mid-1970s, a time when Dave Letterman also worked for Indianapolis radio stations such as WIBC-AM. One time on the air at WIBC, he announced the fake "sale" of the Soldiers and Sailors Monument in downtown Indianapolis to a foreign country that planned to paint it green as a giant tribute to asparagus.

Many Hoosiers were outraged at the joke about the monument—and in an interview years later, Letterman said they had reason to be upset.

"A lesson I've had to learn over and over again in my life, I'm sorry to say, is that just because I may think something is funny doesn't mean it's funny to everyone else," he said.

"People called the radio station very upset because their relatives had given their lives in battle for this country. To them, the Soldiers and Sailors Monument had sincere, symbolic significance."

His experiences in Indianapolis TV and radio stations obviously helped prepare Letterman for the big time. But the Hoosier comedian, who was born in 1947, said the true "turning point" in his life came during his years at Broad Ripple High School.

That turning point happened while he had an after-school job as a stock boy at Atlas Supermarket, a job he took when he quit the freshman (reserve) basketball team at Broad Ripple.

"I was tired of it, and I knew I wasn't that good," Letterman recalled in the interview. "My parents very wisely said, 'Fine. You can quit. But if you give that up, you have to get a job. We don't want you loafing after school.'

"To this day, the Atlas experience remains one of the most positive influences of my life. It was the first time I was entrusted with real responsibility."

After graduating from Broad Ripple High in 1965, Letterman studied radio and TV at Ball State University. He became known on campus for his pranks. One Saturday afternoon, fifty-two members of a fraternity were crowded into a TV lounge to watch the Indiana high school basketball championship.

Young Dave convinced a buddy to drive a pickup truck to the opposite side of the fraternity house. Then, from the bedrooms on the upper floor, other friends tossed all of the mattresses—fifty-two of them!—out a window. Letterman and his friends stacked the mattresses on the truck and drove off. They hid the mattresses several miles from campus in a barn at a friend's farm. Meanwhile, the confused fraternity members had to sleep on the springs of their bed frames—for an entire week!

Letterman has conceded that he wasn't the best student in college. Since becoming famous and wealthy (in 1993, he signed a $14 million contract with CBS), Letterman has given thousands of dollars to Ball State—including money for scholarships and a new radio and TV station for students.

During the 1980s and early '90s, Letterman struggled to find the right TV program to showcase his humor. Some of his shows, including a morning program, were canceled. He became popular on a late-late talk show full of wild routines. On one show, Dave put on a Velcro suit and flung himself against a wall. He stuck! But in 1992, he was passed over to be the host of NBC's *The Tonight Show*; Jay Leno got the gig instead.

Fortunately for Letterman, his new show on CBS—broadcast from the Ed Sullivan Theater in New York City—took off with a bang. Millions of Americans loved his regular segments such as "Stupid Pet Tricks." (On one show, a dog used his paws to open a refrigerator door and bring cool drinks to his owner.)

In early 2000, Dave Letterman made headlines around the world for a serious reason. He suddenly had to have a major heart operation—quintuple-bypass surgery—to save his life.

When Letterman taped his "comeback" TV show after his surgery, he fought back tears as he thanked his doctors and nurses. Typically, he also added a quip. Letterman said he had a quintuple (five)—not double—bypass because the hospital had a "special" on bypass surgeries that week.

Other stars of today from Indiana

Shelley Long

This actress from **Fort Wayne** is best known for her leading role as Diane, a snobby waitress on the popular TV series *Cheers*. **Shelley Long** (who was born in 1949) won an Emmy Award for *Cheers*, on which she starred from 1982 to 1987; the comedy series is still popular in reruns. Long also has starred in several movies, including light comedies such as *The Money Pit* (1986) with Tom Hanks and *Troop Beverly Hills* (1989), about a Girl Scout troop of wealthy girls. In the movie version of *The Brady Bunch* (1995), Long updated the "Mrs. Brady" role made famous on TV by another Hoosier actress, Florence Henderson. (As a high school student in Fort Wayne, Long competed in speech contests against another future TV star, Jane Pauley of Indianapolis.)

Greg Kinnear

He's a cheerful, boyish-looking movie actor and TV personality who was born in **Logansport**, Indiana, in 1963. **Greg Kinnear** spent his summers at a cabin on Lake Wawasee until his family moved overseas when his dad was a diplomat to Lebanon and Greece. Regarded as one of the most likable actors in today's Hollywood, Kinnear had his first major movie role in *Sabrina* (1995), playing a carefree kid brother. His other movies have included *Mystery Men* (1999), in which he portrayed a handsome superhero named Captain Amazing, and the romantic comedy *You've Got Mail* (1997) with Tom Hanks. For his performance in *As Good As It Gets* (1997), Kinnear was nominated for an Academy Award as Best Supporting Actor.

Vivica A. Fox

She has gone from Arlington High School in **Indianapolis** to Hollywood as a top movie actress of the early twenty-first century. **Vivica A. Fox** (who was born in 1964) soared to fame in blockbuster movies such as *Independence Day* (1996), which was about an alien invasion of Earth. In *Batman & Robin* (1997), she played a villainess named "Ms. B. Haven". (Get it? The name sounds like "misbehavin'.") Her other movies have included *Soul Food* (1997). That same year, she was chosen as one of the "Fifty Most Beautiful People in the World" by *People* magazine. And in late 2000, Fox appeared as a guest celebrity on the hugely popular TV show *Who Wants To Be A Millionaire?* (At Arlington High School, Vivica A. Fox was known as "Angie." That's her middle name.)

Hoosiers behind the scenes

Some of the most popular musicals in movie history have been directed by **Robert Wise**. He was the director of *The Sound of Music* (1965), which tells the story of the real-life Von Trapp family of singers. The movie, which features songs such as *My Favorite Things* and *Do Re Mi*, set box office records. Wise also directed *West Side Story* (1961), a musical about teenage gangs in New York City. (That movie won ten Academy Awards, and one of the Oscars went to Robert Wise as Best Director.) His long list of credits also includes directing *The Day the Earth Stood Still* (1951), a science fiction classic about a friendly alien who comes to Earth to urge people to live in peace.

So what is Wise's connection to Indiana?

Shelley Long. (Photofest)

Vivica A. Fox. (Photofest)

Greg Kinnear. (Photofest)

Robert Wise was born in Winchester, Indiana, in 1914. Before going to Hollywood, he attended Connersville High School and Franklin College.

Another Hoosier made his mark behind the scenes in Hollywood, but as a writer, not as a director.

Steve Tesich of **East Chicago**, Indiana, won an Academy Award for writing a joyous movie set in Indiana. *Breaking Away* (1979) was filmed in **Bloomington**; the movie is about a group of free-spirited teenagers who attempt to win the legendary "Little 500" bicycle race at Indiana University.

Tesich, who was born in 1942, was an avid bicyclist. He based *Breaking Away* on his experiences on the IU campus and in a "Little 500" race during the early 1960s.

Sadly, Tesich died suddenly of a heart attack at age fifty-three in 1996. He had written several plays and other movies, including *Four Friends* (1981), which is set in northwestern Indiana. In an interview a few years before his death, Steve Tesich called Indiana his "spiritual home."

Florence Henderson

Millions of people know Florence Henderson from her role as "Mrs. Brady," the cheerful mom on TV's *The Brady Bunch* series. There she is on the TV screen in reruns today, managing to smile as she and the Brady family's housekeeper, Alice, deal with constant chaos in a household of six children and a dog named Tiger.

Even though *The Brady Bunch*, a comedy show about a blended family, originally ran for only five years (1969–1974), it has been broadcast continually ever since because its reruns are so popular. As a result, Florence Henderson is identified permanently with the image of a perfect mom, always warm and perky.

But Henderson (1934–) struggled through plenty of rough days when she was a girl in southern Indiana. The youngest of ten children, Florence Henderson was born in the town of **Dale** to a family that was known as "dirt poor." Her parents were sharecroppers on tobacco farms; that is, they didn't own the land, but just worked the fields for meager pay. Sometimes little Florence helped out in the fields. Her job, she recalled years later, was to pick the insects off the tobacco leaves.

At the Catholic schools that Henderson attended in southern Indiana,

Florence Henderson, the eternal "Mrs. Brady." (Courtesy of *The Indianapolis Star*)

the girls were required to wear uniforms. Because of her family's poverty, Henderson often showed up in ragtag versions. Humiliated, she made up stories about "accidents" to explain her tattered clothes.

"The nuns knew my family situation," she said. "But they never hurt my pride, for which I am extremely grateful."

There was at least one bright spot: Family members and neighbors noticed that young Florence Henderson had a beautiful singing voice.

"I used to go to the corner store as a little girl, sit on the counter, and sing my heart out for coins," she said years later. "I guess I'm still singing for my supper."

Impressed with her talent, family friends paid for Henderson to move to New York City after high school. She became a Broadway star in musical such as *Fanny* (1954) and *The Girl Who Came to Supper* (1963).

However, Henderson realizes she will always be remembered primarily for *The Brady Bunch*. She considered the role of "Mrs. Brady" to be ideal for her. During the series, she was raising her own four children—who were about the same age as the Brady kids.

Why is the show so popular? Florence has a theory. She says many children identify with the TV series because they, too, live in families with stepparents, half-brothers, stepsisters or other "blended" relationships.

Fun facts

- Florence Henderson has had two, widely separated relationships with *The Today Show*, one of the longest-running programs in TV history. For about one year (1959–1960), she was a regular hostess on the morning news and talk show. Nearly forty years later, beginning in 1999, she became the co-host of *Later Today*, a talk show that followed *Today* on NBC-TV.
- The 400,000 people who attend the Indianapolis 500 have seen Florence Henderson every May since the early 1980s. At the Indianapolis Motor Speedway, she sings "America" just before the command of "Gentlemen, start your engines" that begins the world-famous race.
- Florence Henderson's birthday is February 14—Valentine's Day.

David Anspaugh and Angelo Pizzo

When they were college roommates and fraternity brothers at Indiana University in the late 1960s, David Anspaugh and Angelo Pizzo used to roam around Bloomington, making experimental films.

Now they make major movies seen around the world; some of their films' plots have been inspired by true Indiana sports stories. Anspaugh (1945–), who grew up in Decatur in northeastern Indiana, is a director. His former roommate, Pizzo (1948–), a Bloomington native, is a screenwriter.

The duo's best-known movie, *Hoosiers* (1986), was based on the most famous moment in Indiana high school basketball history. A team from tiny Milan, a town in southern Indiana, beat basketball teams from much larger schools in bigger cities and surprised the entire state by winning the championship in 1954. The movie *Hoosiers*, which was filmed in Indiana, has been praised as a classic about small-town life and as one of the best sports movies ever made.

The second movie that Anspaugh and Pizzo made together was *Rudy* (1993). Filmed at the University of Notre Dame, it was based on the true story of a boy who dreamed of playing football for Notre Dame's team, always among the best in the nation.

Movie director David Anspaugh. (Courtesy of *The Indianapolis Star*)

Screenwriter Angelo Pizzo, and with author Nelson Price during the filming of *Rudy* on the Notre Dame campus in 1992. (Both courtesy of *The Indianapolis Star*)

The title character, Rudy, was told for years that he wasn't good enough either to attend Notre Dame or to make the Fighting Irish football team; he suffered from dyslexia, a reading disorder, and was considered too short for college football. Despite all of that, Rudy never gave up. He eventually was accepted into Notre Dame and astonished his critics by making a crucial play in the final twenty-seven seconds of the last game of his senior year.

"I'm determined to make movies that I would want to see," Angelo Pizzo says. "I know this state. I know the people. I know the feelings here."

John Mellencamp

He was born in a small town. He sings and writes about small towns. And he lives in a small town.

Rock star **John Mellencamp**—often called "rock music's poet of the American heartland"—is as thoroughly Hoosier as any famous person from Indiana. Mellencamp (who was born in 1951) has lived in the state his entire life and often takes up causes to help people in the Midwest. To call attention to the struggles of Midwestern farmers, Mellencamp and country music star Willie Nelson organized the first Farm Aid concert in 1985.

By then, Mellencamp was world famous thanks to his album *American Fool*. It racked up sales of three million in 1982, making it the biggest-selling album of the year. Several of the hit songs from the album—including "Jack and Diane" and "Hurt So Good"—are frequently played on radio stations and at sporting events to this day. Some of Mellencamp's later hit songs, particularly "Lonely Ol' Night" and "Pink Houses," describe the dreams and frustrations of residents of small towns in the Midwest.

Mellencamp grew up in **Seymour**, a town in southern Indiana. His father, Richard, was an electrician who became vice president of an electric company. His mother, Marilyn, had

John Mellencamp, rock music singer and songwriter. (Photofest)

been a runner-up in the Miss Indiana pageant before she married Richard. John Mellencamp attended Seymour High School and, for a time, Vincennes University; he was still a teenager when he married for the first time.

Also as a teenager, Mellencamp began playing the guitar in rock bands and writing music. In 1975, he was signed by a manager who wanted to "remake" the Hoosier singer. The manager billed Mellencamp under the flashy name "Johnny Cougar" and

encouraged him to dress as a glittery teen idol. Mellencamp hated all of that, and his first album failed.

Fortunately, a song on his second album, "Ain't Even Done With the Night," became a hit. Mellencamp then topped himself with the *American Fool* album of 1982.

He's been a star ever since, almost always performing to huge crowds around the country. Unlike many famous people who move to California or New York, Mellencamp has chosen to continue to live in his home state.

Mellencamp and his third wife, fashion model Elaine Irwin-Mellencamp, live in Bloomington. His recording studio is located nearby in Brown County, in the small town of Belmont. (Belmont is the same beautiful town where famous painter T. C. Steele lived about eighty years earlier. See the section about him earlier in this book.)

Many of Mellencamp's albums—which include *Uh-Huh* (1984), *Scarecrow* (1985) and *Mr. Happy Go Lucky* (1996)—feature instruments seldom heard in rock music: violin, accordion, mandolin and dulcimer.

A sports lover since boyhood, Mellencamp is an avid fan of Indiana University's teams. He has donated more than $1.5 million to IU for an indoor athletic facility.

Although he looks youthful and slender, Mellencamp is a grandfather. He has three grown daughters from his early marriages: Michelle, Teddi Jo, and Justice. He and Elaine also have two young sons, Hud and Speck.

John Mellencamp cut back on his touring and began spending a lot more time in Bloomington with his family after suffering a heart attack in 1994. He was only forty-two years old when the heart attack occurred.

Mellencamp has called that health crisis the "wake-up call" that helped him lead a calmer lifestyle.

Other rock and pop music stars from Indiana

The Jackson Five

There were nine children in the family of Gary residents Joe and Katherine Jackson. Several of these children—particularly Michael and Janet—have become famous around the world as solo performers in pop music.

First, though, five of the Jackson brothers became famous as the Jackson Five. (Actually, there were six brothers who performed—with one brother replacing another.) Their debut (first, or introductory) song, "I Want You Back," was a smash hit around the world in 1970. More attention followed thanks to an album called *Diana Ross Presents the Jackson Five*. (Ross is a superstar pop singer who is credited with helping launch the Jackson Five's career.)

So how *did* the Jackson Five get started?

Their father, Joe Jackson, operated a crane at a steel mill in Gary, but money was tight for the family. When Joe and mother Katherine noticed that their young sons had musical talent, they searched for places in the Gary area where the brothers could perform. The original Jackson Five consisted of the five oldest brothers: Jackie (born in 1951), Tito (born in 1953), Jermaine (born in 1954), Marlon (born in 1957), and, of course, Michael (born in 1958).

Tito persuaded his brothers to form a group, and they entertained at nightspots and talent competitions in northwestern Indiana and in Chicago. Their big break came in the mid-1960s when Michael was nine years old. The brothers performed at a rally for Richard Hatcher, Gary's longtime mayor. They impressed some music industry officials who were in the crowd. Soon the brothers were signed to a contract with Motown Records of Detroit.

The first change among the brothers occurred in 1976, when Jermaine Jackson left the group. He was replaced by the youngest brother, Randy (born in 1962).

Meanwhile, Michael Jackson had begun an enormously successful solo career. Michael was just thirteen years old when he had his first hit, "I'll Be There," in 1972. By then, the Jackson family had left Indiana for California.

The popularity of the Jackson Five eventually declined, but Michael has remained in the headlines for many reasons. In 1982, he released *Thriller*, which became the biggest-selling album in history at the time.

The Jackson Five in 1972 (from left): Marlon, Jackie, Michael, Jermaine, and Tito. (Photofest)

Two of Michael's sisters, LaToya (born in 1956) and Janet (born in 1966), also have enjoyed success in solo singing and/ or acting careers since the family moved to California.

Babyface

A boy who grew up in Indianapolis went on to become a pop music "hit machine" in the 1990s. Babyface—whose real name is Kenneth Edmonds—has turned out nearly twenty Number One—and one hundred Top Ten—records as a singer, songwriter, or producer since 1987.

Known as "Kenny" to his boyhood Hoosier friends, Edmonds (born in 1958) graduated from North Central High School in 1976. As a teenager, he played guitar and sang as a counselor at central Indiana summer camps. He also performed as a teen at local nightspots with a band called Tarnished Silver.

Some of Babyface's hit songs include "I Love You Babe" (1987) and "When Can I See You" (1994). In 1997, he was nominated for twelve Grammy Awards. That tied a record set by his boyhood idol, Gary native Michael Jackson.

Edmonds and his wife, Tracey, have two sons, Brandon and Dylan. The family lives in southern California.

Crystal Gayle

Pop and country singer Crystal Gayle grew up in Wabash, a town in northern Indiana. Her best-known song, "Don't It Make My Brown Eyes Blue," was a huge hit in the mid-1970s; she won a Grammy Award for her recording of it.

Crystal Gayle. (Photofest)

Babyface in a studio pose (top); and with his mother, Barbara Edmonds (right), and Indiana Governor and Mrs. Frank O'Bannon in 1999 at a ceremony during which a portion of Interstate 65 was renamed "Kenneth 'Babyface' Edmonds Highway." (Both courtesy of Indiana Black Expo)

Crystal Gayle (her real name is Brenda Gail Webb) was born in Kentucky in 1951. She was just three years old when her family moved to Indiana. (Meanwhile, her older sister Loretta Lynn became a famous country singer identified with Kentucky.) Gayle graduated from Wabash High School and sang in clubs in Bloomington before becoming a star.

Now she lives near Nashville, Tennessee, a city known as the country music capital. Gayle says that she and her husband, who grew up in Logansport, Indiana, always consider themselves Hoosiers.

In early 2001, Gayle recorded an album of songs for children, *In My Arms*. She donated a portion of the proceeds from the album to DreamMakers Inc., an organization dedicated to granting the wishes of children with life-threatening diseases.

Bibliography

Bird, Larry. *Bird Watching: On Playing and Coaching the Game I Love*. New York: Warner Books, 1999.

Boomhower, Ray E. *But I Do Clamor: May Wright Sewall, A Life*. Zionsville, Indiana: Guild Press of Indiana, 2001.

Bundles, A'Lelia Perry. *Madam C. J. Walker: Entrepreneur*. Philadelphia: Chelsea House, 1991.

Caldwell, Howard. *Tony Hinkle: Coach for All Seasons*. Bloomington, Indiana: Indiana University Press, 1991.

Diller, Daniel C. and Stephen L. Robertson. *The Presidents, First Ladies and Vice Presidents*. Washington, D.C.: Congressional Quarterly Press, 2001.

Gordon, Jeff, with Bob Zeller. *Jeff Gordon: Portrait of a Champion*. New York: Harper Horizon, 1998.

Hall, Patricia. *Johnny Gruelle: Creator of Raggedy Ann and Andy*. Gretna, Louisiana: Pelican Publishing Co., 1993.

Harris, Warren G. *Gable & Lombard*. New York: Simon and Schuster, 1974.

Lewis, Jeff. *The Sweetheart of Sigma Chi: Dave Letterman, the College Years*. Zionsville, Indiana: Guild Press of Indiana, 1997.

Raffert, Stewart. *The Miami Indians of Indiana*. Indianapolis: Indiana Historical Society, 1996.

Robertson, Oscar. *The Art of Basketball*. Cincinnati, Ohio: Oscar Robertson Media Ventures, 1998.

Schaller, Bob. *The Olympic Dream*. Grand Island, Neb.: Cross Training Publishing, 2000.

Terrill, Mashall. *Steve McQueen*. New York: Primus Books, 1993.

Thom, Dark Rain. *Kohkumthena's Grandchildren: The Shawnee*. Zionsville, Indiana: Guild Press of Indiana, 1994.

For an additional bibliography or for more information on many of the figures in *Legendary Hoosiers*, see *Indiana Legends: Famous Hoosiers from Johnny Appleseed to David Letterman* (Guild Press of Indiana, 1997), also by this author.

Index

A

Adams
  J. Ottis, 129
  Wayman, 128
Ade, George, 133
Alford, Steve, 85, 86
Allen, Joe, 111
Andretti
  Aldo, 95, 96
  John, 95–96
  Mario, 95, 96–98
  Michael, 95, 98
Anspaugh, David, 176
Apple Pie, 3
Appleseed, Johnny, 2–4.
Appomattox Campaign, 25
Armstrong, Neil, 109
Aulby, Mike, 92

B

Babyface. *See* Edmonds, Kenneth
    "Babyface"
Bailey, Damon, 85–86
Baker, David, 140
Ball
  Edmund Burke, 102
  Frank, 102
  George, 102
  Lucius, 102
  William C., 102
Battle of Antietam, 24, 25
Battle of Brawner Farm, 24
Battle of Fallen Timbers, 15
Battle of Gettysburg, 23, 24, 25
Battle of the Thames, 11
Battle of Tippecanoe, 10, 13
Battle of Wilderness, 23, 25
Baxter, Anne, 167
Bayh
  Birch, 44
  Evan, 43–44
Bell, Joshua, 65–66

Ben-Hur, 124–125, 125
Benko, Lindsay, 91
Benny, Jack, 168
Bettenhausen
  Gary, 97
  Tony Jr., 97
  Tony Sr., 97
Bird, Larry, 82–84
Bissot. *See* Vincennes, Sieur(s) de
Blass, Bill, 118
Bolton, Michael, 141
Brown, Mark N., 111
Brown, Mordecai "Three-Finger", 70, 71
Brown, William Lyon, 24
Bryant, Hallie, 61
Bundles, A'Lelia, 33
Bush
  George H. W., 41, 42
  George W., 170

C

Carmichael, Hoagy, 139–141
Carnegie, Tom, 161
Chancellorsville Campaign, 23, 24, 25
Chapman, John. *See* Appleseed, Johnny
Charles, Ray, 141
Chickasaw, 5–6
Clark
  George Rogers, 7–8
  William, 8
Classical School for Girls, 30
Cleveland, Grover, 28
Clinton, Hillary Rodham, 158
Coffin
  Catharine, 20–22
  Levi, 20–22
Colfax, Schuyler, 42
Conner, John, 49–50
Conner, William, 49–50
Counsilman, James "Doc", 93–94
Crowe, Ray, 61
Cruise, Tom, 170

D

Dan Patch, 92–93
Davis, Jim, 114, 121–122
Dean, James, 56–57, 114, 169
Debs, Eugene V., 31–32, 132
DeFrantz, Anita, 90–91
Dillinger, John, 37–38
Dreiser, Theodore, 133–134
Dresser, Paul, 133–134
Dunne, Irene, 166

E

Edmonds, Kenneth "Babyface", 179
Equal Suffrage Society of Indianapolis, 30
Erskine, Carl, 70, 71

F

Fairbanks, Charles W., 42
Faye, Alice, 168
Fisher, Carl, 106–107, 132
Forsyth, William, 129
Fourteenth Indiana Volunteers, 23
Fox
  Michael J., 158
  Vivica A., 172, 173
Fugitive Slave Act of 1793, 22

G

Gardner, Willie, 61
Garfield (the cat), 121–122
Garfield, James, 125
Garrett, Bill, 39, 61
Gayle, Crystal, 179
George
  Jeff, 75–76, 77
  Tony, 107
Gingold, Josef, 66
Gipp, George, 74, 77
Gordon, Jeff, 62–64, 96
Grant, Ulysses S., 24, 25
Graves, Michael, 108

Gregoire, Stephan, 161
Griese
 Bob, 75, 77
 Brian, 77
Grissom, Virgil "Gus", 109, 110
Gruelle
 Johnny, 130
 Richard B., 129
Guerin, Mother Theodore, 148–149

H

Halston, 118
Hamilton, Henry, 7
Hanks, Tom, 172
Hannah, Alexander, 21
Harbaugh, Greg, 109
Harding, Warren G., 31
Harmer, Josiah, 15
Harmon, Tom, 75, 77
Harris, Phil, 168, 169
Harrison
 Benjamin, 13, 26–28, 128
 Caroline, 13, 26, 28
 John, 27
 William Henry, 10, 11, 12–13, 26, 27
Haynes, Elwood, 100
Hays, Will, 164–165
Henderson, Florence, 172, 174–175
Hendricks, Thomas A., 42
Henry, Patrick, 7
Herman, Billy, 70
Hesburgh, Father Theodore, 150–151
Heston, Charlton, 125
Hinkle, Tony, 79
Hodges, Gil, 70, 71
Hulman, Tony, 107

I

Indiana Light Artillery Brigade, 103
Indiana, Robert, 144
Indianapolis Classical School for Boys, 30
Indianapolis Museum of Art, 30
Indianapolis Propylaeum, 30

J

Jackson Five, 178
Jackson
 Janet, 178
 LaToya, 178
 Michael, 68, 178
John, Elton, 68

K

Kekionga, 14
Kennedy, Jacqueline, 118
Kerrigan, Nancy, 158
Kimbrough, Emily, 55
Kinnear, Greg, 172, 173
Knight, Bobby, 80–81, 85
Ku Klux Klan, 35–36

L

Landis, Kenesaw Mountain, 71
Lee, Robert E., 24, 25
Letterman, David, 170–171
Lightning Brigade, 103
Lilly
 Col. Eli, 103–105
 Eli II, 104
 Eli "Mr. Eli", 104
 Josiah Kirby "J. K." III, 104
 Josiah Kirby "J. K." Jr., 104
 Josiah Kirby "J. K." Sr., 103–104
Lincoln, Abraham, 26, 51–53
Little Turtle, 14–15
Lombard, Carole, 164, 165
Long, Shelley, 172, 173
Louganis, Greg, 68
Lugar, Richard, 58–59, 143
Lynn, Loretta, 179

M

Madame Walker Urban Life Center, 34
Main, Marjorie, 166–167
Manning, Peyton, 76–77
Marshall, Thomas R., 42
Masters, Bob, 60
Mattingly, Don, 70, 71
McClure, John, 25
McGinnis, George, 86–87
McQueen, Steve, 165, 166
Meehan, Jeannette Porter, 127
Mellencamp, John, 177–178
Menominee, 18–19
Merrimac, 25
Merriwether, Willie, 61
Miller, Cheryl, 89
Miller, Reggie, 88–89
Monitor, 25
Montgomery, Wes, 140
More, Thomas, 17
Morton, Oliver P., 24

N

Niblack, John, 35, 36
Nicholson, Meredith, 133
Nineteenth Indiana Volunteers, 23–24
Noël, Nancy, 119–120, 130
Norell, Norman, 118

O

Oberholtzer, Madge, 35, 36
Owen
 David Dale, 16, 17
 Robert, 16, 17
 Robert Dale, 16

P

Palmer, Betsy, 169
Parseghian, Ara, 75, 76, 77
Patty, Sandi, 110, 152–153
Pauley, Jane, 158–159, 172
Peanut Butter and Jelly Thumbprint No-
 Bake Popcorn Cookie, 117
Phelps, Jaycie, 91
Pizzo, Angelo, 176
Plump, Bobby, 60, 87
Porter, Cole, 137–138
Prophet (Tenskwatawa), 9–11, 13
Prophetstown, 10, 13
Purvis, Melvin, 38
Pyle, Ernie, 156–157

Q

Quayle
 James Danforth "Dan", 41–42
 Marilyn Tucker, 42

R

Raggedy Ann, 130
Rapp, Johann George, 16
Rappites, 16, 17
Reagan
 Nancy, 118
 Ronald, 77
Redenbacher, Orville, 116–117
Remy, William, 35, 36
Riley, James Whitcomb, 32, 54, 131–133
Robertson, Oscar, 60–61
Rockne, Knute, 74, 76, 77
Roosevelt, Theodore, 133
Ross, Jerry, 110, 111

S

Schenkel, Chris, 161
Second Manassas Campaign, 25
Seven Days Battles, 23, 25
Seventeenth Indiana Volunteers, 28
Sewall, May Wright, 29–30, 128
Seybold
   Natalie "Kim", 92
   Wayne, 92
Sharp, Scott, 97, 106
Shaw, Wilbur, 97
Shriner
   Herb, 168–169
   Kin, 168, 169
   Wil, 168, 169
Skelton, Red, 165–166
Skinner, Cornelia Otis, 55
Slocum, Frances, 46–48
Smith, Asa, 35, 36
Snyderman, Dr. Nancy, 160
Spitz, Mark, 93, 94
Stark, Otto, 129
Steele, T. C., 128–130
Stephenson, D. C., 35–36
Stewart, Tony, 63, 64, 96
Stratton-Porter, Gene, 126–127
Strauss, Juliet V., 54
Streisand, Barbra, 118
Studebaker, 100–101
   Clement, 100, 101, 102
   F. Jacob, 100, 101, 102
   Henry, 100, 101, 102
   John Mohler, 100, 101, 102
   Peter, 100, 101, 102
Sunday, Billy, 153–154

T

Tarkington, Booth, 135–136
Taylor, Marshall W. "Major", 72–73
Tecumseh, 9–11, 13
Tesich, Steve, 173
Tharp, Twyla, 145
Thomas, Kurt, 92, 93
Tipton, John, 18
Trail of Death, 18, 19
Treaty of Fort Wayne, 11, 13
Trudeau, Garry, 159
Trueblood, Elton, 154
Twentieth Indiana Volunteers, 24–25
Twin Lakes, 18, 19

U

Underground Railroad, 20–21
Utopia, 16, 17

V

Van Buren, Martin, 18, 19
Vincennes, Sieur(s) de, 5–6
Vonnegut, Kurt Jr., 142–143
Voss, Janice, 111

W

Wakefield, Dan, 143
Walker
   A'Lelia, 34
   Madam C. J., 33–34
Wallace
   David, 18
   Lew, 124–125
Walters, Barbara, 118, 158
War of 1812, 11, 13
Washington, George, 53
Wayne, Anthony "Mad Anthony", 15
Webb, Clifton, 166, 167
Weber, Richard "Dick", 92
Wells, Herman B, 39–40
West, Jessamyn, 55
White, Ryan, 67–68
Williams, Donald, 111
Willkie, Wendell, 58, 59
Wilson, Woodrow, 133
Wise, Robert, 172–173
Wolf, David, 110–111
Wooden, John, 78–79
Wright
   Orville, 114–115
   Wilbur, 114–115

Z

Zoeller, Fuzzy, 92